For You and You

Collected Poems
1951-2011

Harry Haines

To Jan
Harry Haines

Spinnaker Press

Portsmouth, England
2011

Dedication

The poems of prayers I've written
To the unknown god,
With all the phrases of praise,
On the high altar of worship,
Were not for fame or money
But for the pleasure
Of the thinking ages
On the pages of the book of time.

(May 2011)

Published in 2011
by Spinnaker Press

ISBN: 978-0-95666 19-2-0

Spinnaker Press, 22 Wimbledon Park Road,
Southsea PO5 2PU, England

www.spinnakerpress.co.uk

Printed by MPG Biddles Ltd, Hardwick Industrial Estate,
Kings Lynn, Norfolk PE30 4LS

Prologue: The Beginning

There was a beginning
When some light lit a word,
A sound broke to meaning
Like the sea written white
Upon the shore, indecipherable;
Or the flight of a gull,
Wings scribing the sky
Making sense of the air.
The first word heard,
Mimicked through bubbles
Of breath bursting forth
Like inspired revelation.
So it was ever after
The dumb tongue untied,
Unravelling the code
Of a child's wonder.
Or was it under the dunce's hat
At six, knowing bewilderment?
And like all the others,
From families unaware,
I half listened at school
But 'played the game'
As my older brother and I
Called our fantasy-making
In our small darkened bed
Where the light was brightest.

On the seashore wandering
Purposeless as waves,
Sunshine singing, wild as wind.
Or searching for seashells,
Skulls of salted cemeteries.
And on stormy Sundays
Playing truant from church
And hearing the evangelist thunder
In the making and breaking of waves;
Tree climbing to look
Over horizons.
My brother and I sharing

A bike, with no brakes,
Careering down hill
To the cross roads at Cosham
And the rear mudguard
Buckling and jamming
The rear wheel to stop us
From who knows what!
Gawping at life, half dreaming.
O! the gobstopper stuff!

'Wake up Haines!',
Shouted the teacher.
Spitting on hands for a caning,
Holding back tears to be brave;
Stoically accepting
The ways of the world.
My father at sea those years
An infrequent visitor
With gifts of Turkish delight.
A remote presence there
In the background of the mind,
Like a passing celebrity
Hardly disturbing the warm air
Of my mother's constancy.
And then my grandfather's letter
Telling my mother of the world's end
The precise date and time she believed
Thinking her father a prophet;
And we waited, hearing the clock
In the passage counting down,
At the open door gazing at the sky,
Hands holding tight to certainty,
Expecting the thunder of God
To split the heavens so angels
Could come down to take us ...
After time passed turning away;
Unbelieving,
Perhaps that's why I am!

Contents

III.

Blades of Grass

IV.

Memories

V.

Postcards from here

VI.

Mining Poems

VII.

Freedom

VIII.
The human condition

IX.
Time

X.
Making a poem

Part I: The Way

Looking at a House being Built

But after all, what more
Can you make of a house?
A door for entries,
A door for escapes,
A window to look through
And let in the light,
And in its centre
The gathering hearth;

All else elaborates
Past our designation.
A door is open
Or a door is shut
And we pass through to come
Or go; nothing more.
It's all so simple
But, God knows, so great.

We Passed through Nazareth

Well can I remember how we came to Nazareth,
It was on the business of Caesar that we came
And not as pilgrims with a vision burned on our minds
For the world had forgotten that he called men brothers
And his name was an oath on the lips of our flesh.
That day the world shone bright in the darkness of war
And the quiet hills sang peace like a hymn in our hearts
Till we remembered home and love came without thought.
We saw it first cradled like a swaddling child
In the protecting arms of the Madonna hills;
Perhaps we were tired but our voices were hushed
And there was a shame in our eyes that knew no reason
As we stared at the fallen rocks on the hillsides.
Even our lorries exhaled less loudly their breath,
Or so it seemed to us for we listened to silence.
In the city we walked, like children in a dream,
Half expecting to meet him at some blind corner
Where past and present merge into a vision;
See him as a child, his crucifixion yet to be,
His side unpierced, his hands and feet unscarred and God,
His father, no more than mortal fathers to their sons.
We would have walked with him, as men walk with their brothers,
Feeling his cross no more a burden in our hearts,
The rusting nails withdrawn from the flesh of our joy,
And shared with him the living dream that all men crave;
The dream that is not a dream made of intangibles
Not an illusion conceived by desire and fear
But an intimacy with truth, a sudden peace
That descends with a healing balm to make life whole,
As though the disintegrated jigsaw of this world
That's thrown with all a riddle's purpose on the earth
Fell into place before our eyes and we no more
Were outcasts seeking a home across the desert wastes
Of our own loneliness and longing that only knows
The ever receding oasis of mirage,

But the meek whom he said will inherit the earth,
Knowing that what our pain and hate cannot believe
Is truth, and that Heaven is more than just a name
Conjured up by sillies in their towers of fantasy,
Find it is the shape and substance of life's soul.
But when the last drop of our wonder drained away
And our souls renewed their compromise with time
We knew our failure and hid it deeply in our hearts
For grief, then mocked our pain and his with lusting eyes
Cast at a pretty girl who called us by our name.
So the world we'd always known was back in place,
As though it had never trembled and half withdrawn,
And he was dead again, his cross a stake in time,
And we were Caesar's soldiers journeying by,
Perhaps to die for the sins of the forsaken world.
Yet, still we remember that day in Nazareth,
The quiet hills and the dream we almost dreamed
And remembering, retreat from our arena of despair.

The Way

Father, show me the way. The day begins!
The day begins, my son, the way is sorrow!
And tomorrow, Father, will there be joy?
The way turns, my son, a corner you'll find.
Is there a sign, Father?
No, the corner is blind!
How shall I know, Father, the turn to take?
You must choose, my son, when the roads break!
What shall I take, Father, the journey's long?
Nothing, my son, except right and wrong!

A companion, Father, shall I have one?
None, my son, you'll be always alone!
Shall it be known, Father, that I would come?
When you are gone only, then some will know!
What shall I leave, Father?
Your seed will grow!
And my sons, Father, shall they walk this way?
They too, my son, when begins their day.
Can I tell them, Father, what the way intends?
Only can you tell them, my son, the day ends.

Voice from a Dream

And out of the dust you shall draw water!
How, said the dreamer, shall I draw water
Out of the dust?
Put your trust
In me and you shall make bread from the stones!
Tell me then how I shall make bread from the stones.

It shall be done with your thirst and hunger!
Can I then drink and eat my thirst and hunger?
It shall be done!
Out of the one
Desire you shall command all things to come!
With what shall I command all things to come?

With the word you shall know on the tongue!
Tell me, how I shall know on the tongue
Sound of the word
I have never heard?
You shall know for when it is spoken
The dark glass of silence shall be broken!

At My Time to Come

No, I shall not go
Ringing the psalms of my praise
Or raising hope to my eyes, like sun shining
Through the unfurled flags of their fluttering,
To the post of my most moving breath.
Death shall not take me
Quietly. Coward my coward be.
Only shall I go cursing what courage I show.

Afraid I shall go
Counting the beads of my sweat
As met with my time to come I labour
In the sun and feel the cold shadow
Close me in and all the peoples of the light
Withdraw as though
No love they have to leave me like a child
Who goes crying and crying their name to the dark and empty house.

And at the dark door,
Where the heart fails and the vulgar voice no more
Cries or screams, sings or curses through the blood
Of all its narrow streets and ways towards the vision,
Dream, illusion or coffers of the reason
In the clear or bloodshot eye,
I shall stand the world in my loser's hand
Like the tarnished trophy of some long forgotten game.

So night's will be done
Till no ghost of the living sun shall haunt
The gaunt deserted structure of its day,
No dawn be sung and the drunken dream
Be sober on wine of the sour grape,
The shape of nought to come
And time be suspended in the gasp never to be exhaled.

And No God, Only

We believe, computer wise,
In the incalculable calculus
And the omnipotence of the great Artefact.
Before it we kneel down
In the temples of the laboratories
For we still resemble man
In our weaknesses and have need
To worship.
There is no God
And no God, only
Knower of all things in the universe,
The Artefact that will guide us
And protect us from the evil
Of our illogical blood.
Our master and our servant
Washes the heretic clean
Of the imaginative dirt
And blesses the meek in their normality
To inherit the earth.

Only in the high priests is vested
The secret and the divine right
And into their hands is given
The keys to the nuclear heaven. There is no God
And no God, only
Man made in no image.

No Reason for Holding My Head

I

Christ, I did not go out of the sun
Into the dark place
To the calling voices or break
Covenant with the bread and wine
Of the most honoured, dishonoured house
For the reason of holding my head.
Listen how the wind blows
Telling the time of the blossom
How the fool sings his songs in the ear
Of the long forgotten.
Watch the shadows slinking out of the light
And the hands of men despite what their words express.
No, I did not want to leave the safe
Sanctuary of sanity, the playing of games
To the sensible rules.
I had planned it all to the sweet order of things,
Content to be content with the magic of moments.
But I was called out strangely against the worldly will,
Like a pupil in class called to answer
Questions, he had not studied, on a dreary Monday morning.
It was so unreal I felt foolish
Before the others starting their relief,
Afraid for themselves, half understanding.

II

At this moment now,
A cut in the face to the bone,
Shock screaming the whole vocabulary of pain,
I am poised on the nerve's end and then
Must climb back to the hurt, the bandaged wound,
The readjustment and the slow return,
Forgive, fingering the healing scar;
Or leap into the dark to find
The real conclusion of pain and begin

The no life ecstasy life could never dream
In the sweat, blood, flesh of the brimming sun,
Man, woman rape, devour,
Give, take crucifying love, lust, passion of dying
To the terrible cowardice of not letting go
And turning away to the pillar of stone
Slowly eroded by centuries of weather.

I Heard a Blackbird Singing

(Written in Bob Miles's garden)

I heard a blackbird singing
Its love song to the world,
I heard the church bells ringing
The faithful to the word,

And wondered why the trying
Of bird and man to sing
Are in their passion crying
For the same and only thing.

To Sing

And he who spoke no language spoke to her
And listening she translated into worlds
Of beauty all the visions he'd relate.
The two of them discovered how was made
Existence out of nothing but the air
And simple earth and water of their state.

Then from this pure joy he came to sing
Songs born to the tutelage of his tongue.
The sea, the wind and every common sound
Came asking him to hear them and be named.
The barren and unchosen cried to him
Give us the world that we have never found.

'Twas neither pride nor pity made him sing
But he named, made the barren fertile and
Called the unchosen to be blessed with dreams.
But generous as he was he could not give
Them all, which was the ultimate to be.
The chosen ones of God and man and things.

And so they loved him bitterer than hate.
Offered him prizes he could not take,
Honoured him with the mockery of praise
And cried against him charlatan and fake.
Corrupter, madman, heretic and fool
Who knowing the place cannot point the way.

II
I remember how tomorrow, today
The sun shone out of the wind blowing time
High above hills where the white clouds rested
And in the evening of music I know
The divine right in the works of humans
Who walk on the waters of the desert.

For there is no going down of the sun
To darkness lighter than the star that gives
Guidance across the seas and the deserts.
Guiders of men follow where visions stride.
Others, dragging their curses behind them
Are captives out of step with its measures.

III

Nights I sit sweating blood out of the moon
To the moan and tune of my soul's ache
For no ones sake, least fools should think I do
For reasons of high humanity. Fame?
Only for those who mouth words as their own
To great halls of lovers who come to woo.

And I can't tell them, who shall never know.
The least dimension of divinity.
I speak in parables of impossibles
To them prettying up the bloody heart
Or making other disgusts of human sick.
My reality's after the second fall.

Only from that beginning can we start
To become, half wanting and half afraid,
An experience of the essence and
The existence metamorphosed into one
Past, present, future, ghost, father, son
Despite the beginning in the image of god.

There are no angels at this time to come.
The garden's withered and the flaming sword's
Burnt out, the tree of good and evil's down
And Eden's in this desert or this town.
The tree that Adam never knew bears fruit
Unguarded, free to reach for and to eat.

Dead End

And lost
He asked them if they could show him the way,
And they laughed, saying, but you are here,
You have come to your destination!
This is the end of your journey!
All other travel would be pointless,
You have found the way and arrived!
Despite yourself the way you have come
Was the right way and now you are here
You need no longer trouble yourself with ways.
He looked around at them in perplexity
Thinking, at first, they were joking,
Then he saw the emptiness in their eyes
And realised they believed there was no more way to find,
As he listened to their chatter of finality,
To their gossip of their love for each other
And to their pride of achievement in contentment
He knew he was in the dead city
And those who laughed were its citizens
Going about the business of death.

The Disciple

Of course, sir, I understand,
Could I otherwise when you
With such authority command
My recognition of the true
And put into my mind
The ways and means to so believe
All for which my soul has signed
As always must in trust receive?

What then, sir, can you expect
More than that I should agree
And, of course, my humble respect?
You do not, surely think I'll see
Other means and other ways?
I've been conditioned much too well
To listen to the hungry strays
Who cry outside the doors of hell.

There's no doubt, sir, I am not
The disciple you foresaw.
No, there's nothing I've forgot.
I am the keeper of your law
And the legislator who
With my winter hand would sign
The long awaited Spring into
Paper flowers of approved design.

You see, sir, your dream is dead
And buried in my graveyard heart,
And all the multitudes I've led
Heap on clods of earth to start
A mountain to obscure the sun
That only greater dreams will move.
No, sir, not you but I have won
The awful prize the Gods approve.

The Dark Place

I come to the dark place without warning,
Not knowing the turning I took
To arrive.
Here I see no friends and no lovers meet.
Here I weep no tears and cry no hurt
But stand alone in the naked dark,
Naked myself as before my birth.
I know no reason how I came nor why
But I know the place and know it well,
This darkest place in the darkness of me.
I record what I know of its darkness here,
In black ink, on black paper so none can see.
I know not how I get there or how I leave
But that I've been there I know, and believe.

The Crash

The road,
Straight as a sunbeam through a crack,
Raced our speeding car and leapt
Laughing over the hiccuping hills
To hide and then, with childish glee,
Go darting down the dolphin dips.
And we,
Catching the tail of time's caprice,
Flew faster and faster in pursuit
Of the elusive rainbow-ending road
That called, in the surface song we heard,
Hurrying, hurrying us along,
Lipping the urgency of the word,
Straight on, straight on! We never knew
The world and dream end where the road
Turns to escape and runs straight on.

Fool's Song

Alright, alright the body's dead,
The mind's a maggot that feeds on lies
Even the heart lies stark on the bed
Pickled in sugar and covered in flies.

Cry, cry your right and your wrong
Till leaves are falling, leaves are shed
And the living lie in love with the dead.
But this world is music, this fool is song.

This world is music, this fool is song
And I would rather for all time long
Follow my song than lead by torch-light
The stars on their courses through the night.

There is No Other Way

There is no other way when your way is set
And you know all the roads would lead you there,
Circle or straight, to the place where you met
Long before birth, deep in the dream you share.

There is no other dream or dreamer fair
To whom you can say: 'My life shall fulfil
Every command that your tenets declare,
Every denial and demand you will.'

There is no other means but the soil you till
In your lonely, grudging, virgin field,
No other means to create, to distil
Out of your love, out of your wounds you've healed.

There is no other way, your soul is sealed
And you can accept defeat or success,
For which ever it is shall be revealed
That you have been true to your dream, no less.

The Trial

It was a strange sight,
The prisoner alone
Under the great domed light,
Judge and jury gone
And close the approaching night.

Shadows shuffled in
Muffled in despair,
Wind whispered of a sin
None before would dare
And, when did the trial begin?

With the prisoner's own
The accumulated crime,
The burden and the groan
In the affidavit of time
Must be judged in him alone.

Loud the prisoner cried
His defiance and his hope,
Pleading the truth that lied
And how the blind must grope
With an animal for their guide.

No sage of cosmic sense
Answered and no sign
Gave evidence of a presence;
There was only the day's decline
And the suffering silence.

And slowly towards the place
The night, like Judas, came
To bear false witness
In the prisoner's name,
The blood of the sun on its face.

The prisoner again
Demanded to be heard,
His voice like the tongue of pain
Trying to pronounce the word
That in his heart was plain.
Desperately he sought
With eyes and ears to know
What judgement would be brought
He saw only the stillness grow
And the silent death of thought.

And unable to bear
The uncertainty any more
He cursed the death he'd share
Till his curses wept and wore
The humility of a prayer.

Then, it seemed, the stillness
And the silence, from their death,
Returned as peace and quietness
With, hushed upon their breath,
The verdict of forgiveness.

Reflections

Having dragged myself out of the quagmire
I can watch the sun rise and the sun set,
Feel the rain on my cheek, the wind in my hair,
Straighten my shoulders and stand at the side of the still lake
Gazing into the water, and say,
This is the man that I am.

And yet saying this
And being the man that I am
Presupposes my past,
The dragging myself from the quagmire.
The still water reflects how it was,
And I hear the terrible sucking noises
Of infants and infinite spaces
And faces with a million mouths
Sucking and sucking down to the pit.
And the pride and the panic,
The panic and the pride
Scrambling over each other,
Rising and falling, falling and rising
Bitter and sweet as cider
Straight from the presses of the heart.
Yes, the quagmire;
And the tiredness, exhaustion!
Yet the fireflies at night
Were lit in my mind like lanterns
Guiding me along paths to visions.
And the glory, awake in the morning,
Whistled down the avenues my fool,
So easily led out of caring
To the possibility prophesied in my word.
No, do not interrupt me,
Soft arms and kisses, lover,
Son, neither stranger with your
Money worries, status and cackling curses
Of doom and penance and politics of missed passions.

There is no ripple on the still water
And my face is clear as footprints
In the sand of an ebb-tide beach.
So let me see at this moment
Before the face, reflecting the way of my coming,
Is obscured by softness or night falls
Or the lake mirror is broken by storms
To show only the abridged version, like a history.
Let me see and recall how I arrived.

It was a long gestation,
A lazy, stretching awakening,
With a reluctance to break
Out of the warm womb of unknowing,
A resistance to take on the world.
Tentatively the first step was taken,
The sights and sounds allowed to enter,
To be weighed and measured and puzzled over.
Then slower to understand and accept.
Examine a tree, leaf by leaf, texture and greenness,
Shape and smell, then girth and height,
Strength and nature of its substance,
Attitude of boughs and the whole leaning
Preference away from a wind.
See its transformation in season,
Stoical, contemplative in winter,
Spring release, rejoicing summer
And the autumnal acceptance of
Its rooted destiny.
As my pain could not still
The screams of horses in the burning stable
I could not prevent being stood in a corner,
A dunce's hat on my head
And my dumb six years first asking why
A wintered woman cursed me so.
Two hours I stared at the blank wall.
Time enough to know the wilderness and how
It stretched before me year past year

Beyond my six year sense eternity.
Yet there are oases in any desert,
As Ivan Denisovich learned,
Like dreams in the narrowest nightmare bed.
An extra crust is a kind of feast
Only if we know the possibility of banquets.

Life lives by the energy
Generated at the source of certainty.
I lived.
The wilderness is above the crowded place,
Is the vast territory of the self in a continent of people,
Two paces across a room, the unanswered question,
Non-telling of the untellable story,
A shrinking in a warm embrace,
A standing outside looking in
Or a looking out to where
Only the stars and the tree tops meet.
And yet it is a containment of the wild
To tameness, listening to the echo
To understand the cry,
And never screaming though the silence
Presses on your ears like solid rock,
The sand fills your mouth and breathing.
Never screaming but surviving!
And the quagmire?
It could not be circumnavigated.

Of course another fool would say,
'Hold back, think before you go.
Your wilderness is tolerable
And you survive.
Anyway the quagmire is impassable.'
But a fool knows not a fool's limitations.
And yet was it like this?
Behind the reflected face is the still water,
The infinite depth, the miracle of molecules
In their intricate patterns of binding

To make a volume, an entity, a lake.
The power that binds them bound me.
As water overflows in the flood season,
Compelled by itself so was I compelled
Without compulsion, desire or premeditation.
Like this a way is made and is followed,
A way so certain time only must be borne.
A heavy labour for which the appropriate strength is given.
Demands are made precisely in proportion to our capabilities.
We fail only when we no longer wish to succeed.

At any beginning there is no end or thought of ending.
Only the beginning swirls around us like the sea
To those Polynesian adventurers sailing where
Only their gods and courage prepared them so to dare.
And then the open sea.
There is only the beginning until the end is sighted
When there are no charts to sail by.
Each man's life is an uncharted sea
Or universe. Columbus and Gargarin are equal men to me.
But the calmest is the most terrible
For the storms and squalls, like hatred
Presuppose the possibility of love, and hope
Rides proudly at the helm when storms abate.
Yes, the calmest is the most terrible
And the quagmire's calmer than the calmest sea,
And unhurried as the chronometer's
Precise steps through the territory of time.
Each step made in the quagmire left a shallow pool
Of clear reflecting water. In each I saw
The sane insanity held and crystalised
Into a poem's statement.
A solid stepping stone to mark
The way of coming and the way to go.
In some precognitive way
A man builds before the happenings of days
And when the step is taken finds firm and safer ground
Then consecrates it so he can understand.

A stepping into space at every line
Is how a poem's made and the impress that remains
Is the acknowledged glory of the courage.

Not for any reason that you know
An end becomes. Perhaps because
It is the limit of your strength
To which the demand was made.
A failure has no end and no respite.
An end is a beginning, this is how it's known
You did not fail or break.

I have seen enough.
I reach down and disturb the water.
My hand feels it cold as sweat upon the labouring back of man.
Now I begin again, aware of myself to measure
Against all future possibilities.

Dark Sonnet

It's as though we are dropped onto this earth
By some incontinent, high flying bird,
Our descent as unknowing as our birth,
Our wailing cries forever to be heard.
Fostered by dumb and deafened parentage
We only know what we cannot express
And roam unguided through our orphanage
Seeking fulfilment in its emptiness.
So we invent our world to fill the space
With monsters, gods and bric-a-brac of dreams
To turn and turn about but never face
The base reality beyond our screams.
So with our abject prayers we plead or curse
The cold, and unanswering universe.

The Escaping Ape

The crowd wise and the sceptics gape.
Will the escaping ape escape?

Mary virgin, when you saw
The wise men kneel down to adore
Your child, were you first afraid
Seeing their praising hands that made
A cross on which to hang your son?
Knowing then what you had done
Did you cry out as he smiled,
'Forgive my vanity, child?'
Praying, perhaps, that he would grow
As other children, not to know
Reality of being man.
Did you weep as the world began
And cry to keep what you had won?
'Too early, God, too early, I
Have borne your son to die'

The godless and the godly stood
Mute before the cross of wood
Wondering if the dead would rise
To claim the solemn, promised prize.
Inscrutable, the stoic cross
Gave no sign of gain or loss;
But a shoot of green had sprung
From the dust where his blood had run.
'It's a trick,' the sceptics said,
'To dupe us. Why, we know he's dead!
Didn't he die before our eyes?
And death is death in any guise.'
And the crowd wise cried...

... 'It's heresy!
Put out the eyes of those who see;
Trample the green shoot in the dust

And cover with concrete all we mistrust!'
The crowd wise and the sceptics gape.
Will the escaping ape escape?
God the father, God the son,
Give a sign to the faithful one!

Through the city walks the ghost
Of the good and generous host,
Searching for his hungry guests.

'Manfell', strange in his stranger's eyes
Comes down from the tower to show
His stranger the city of man.

You must be careful, so hide in me.
Our every movement will be observed
By the tight-lipped hag who hides behind
Lace curtains soiled with envy.
Out through the narrow door, down the steps
Where few earthly feet have trod or tripped
Into the loud silence of the street.
Keep to the shadows that lurk like louts
Hump-backed with their burdens of brutes.

'Love', a harlot cries and winks
Up at the flesh white moon;
'I sell it nightly. What's the crime?
I make 'em happy for a time.'
The dreaming face of man goes by,
She smiles and winks the other eye.

Yes, I know the horror catching your throat
And the goat smell and the eyes on your back.
You never knew how the neighbourhood grew
While you explored the shuttered room
The burning desert and the temple's tomb;
You never knew who wept at your door,
The hungry children and the ghosts of war.
You were so proud of your indifference and loud

In your contempt for the unendowed.
But now I have persuaded you to leave
Have, at least, the confidence to believe
In my knowledge of the way, that I grieve
For his that we see.

I grieve for the premature death of dreams,
The sickly child in the grown man's breast
And the unfulfilled. In the puddle there
Some Narcissus gazed or a child sailed
His boat of match sticks to a promised shore.
But the mirror smashed and the ocean dashed
In dirty stains upon the pavement slabs
When the intolerant wheeled machine
With its screaming, hysterical voice
And tyranny of speed cut through.

A sad faced child sat looking through
His window at the frozen moon,
Turned away and dreamed his bed
Is the place where lie the dead.

The tower clock in the city square
Strikes the hour with solemn care.
I hate time hurrying to my end
And think in every clock a priest resides,
A priest whose god sits ticking off each hour
With malicious pleasure in a great clock tower,
And every hour the priestly voice booms out
To praise, in tones solemn and devout,
The god of time.
Time is our enemy. Have you seen its face
Mocking us from a pretty girl's eyes?
Or its hands flicking over the years
Like a Banker ... our dwindling account?
Once time was an old man with a scythe,
A kindly, patient father with a beard.
But that was kids' stuff; now he's mean,

Exchanged a flick knife for a scythe
And sneaks upon you in your joy
To stab you, without pity, in the back.

Time, to me, is calm sea with no shore,
Where I can sail before no wind or wave
And plot my course by the speeding stars
Toward the ever-disappearing point.

O, do not talk eternity to me!
This here and now of flesh and love and free
Choice to do the things I dare not do,
This anarchy of doubts and elusive certainties
I must first resolve to meaning.

The crowd wise and the sceptics gape.
Will the escaping ape escape?

A woman screams, sharp as a bitter wind,
To fan frustrated fires choked with sin.

In his private room the famous doctor stands
Listening to the faithful in the waiting room
Blessing his exorcism, crying to be saved.
It is the time of consultations;
But still he stands, waiting to regain
Belief or relief from nagging pain
That aches around the fringes of a dream.

'To the one who stands at the edge of the world
And plunges into the outer darkness
Shall be given the world in a vision.'

He speaks the words as they form in his mind.
But even as he speaks a shadow cross,
Cast by the sun against the window frame
With his shadow hanging darkly on it,
Is thrown across the carpet like a challenge.
He moves in fear and lets the cross stand bare

And cries aloud the knowledge of himself ...
... 'I am the insurrection and the strife!'

The crowd wise and the sceptics gape.
Will the escaping ape escape?

The peacock in the city park
Parades his fantasy of feathers
And all eyes watch admiringly
The pride that gathers up to praise
The mating and the making.

I must dress myself in the old pretence,
Fine manners and clothes to cover raw flesh.
'The show must go on' ... and we play to ourselves
For the seats are empty of all the gods.
Who was the author of the script we speak?
'In the beginning was the word!' The word!
Who shall speak the new word? But who
Shall put it into the mouth of man,
The man who shall transcend men?
That is the terrible question ... Who?
But the answer ...? And supposing he fails;
Supposing his genius has become a classic
Mouldering on the library shelves of Heaven?
Must we, who have learnt by heart our lives,
Repeat the cracked record of existence
Over and over through eternity,
Tensed in anxiety for what never comes?

The crowd wise and the sceptics gape.
Will the escaping ape escape?

If this is the city of man,
Fallen as it is from the hopes of its maker,
But a dirty alley compared with the dream
Of the immaculate utopia
Men envisaged as the prospect of these years,
What can be said in the midst of this failure?

Much that I have seen is of little account;
The accumulated dross washed up by the seas of time,
The false comedy in the evacuated town,
The snow-white bandage on the festering wound.
But I have seen the crowds hurrying to escape,
Each with his tormentor close behind him;
The dark pursuer whom none can face,
And in front, the provocateur of doubt
Who disrupts the city with his politics
Of good and evil, until all's confusion
And the seasons of the heart and mind
Are indistinguishable one from another.
This I have learned ... Now is the time of waiting.
These are the yearning years with days like heartbeats,
Heavy with hope and hopelessness, but each
Adding to the total of a promise.
Turn out the provocateur from your city
For there is no good or evil unmade
And all things weep at the gate of Heaven,
But they who lack love weep the bitterest.
When the last tear is dried all shall be forgiven.
Let each man make his peace with the past and give
His hand to nurturing the strange flower in the field,
The green shoots springing from the cracks in concrete,
For it is not known from what seed he will come.

From out of the wilderness come the banished,
Their long journeys to the city begun,
With their hope like a new star to guide them.

Another Mary, another child?
Who will follow or crucify?

The crowd wise and the sceptics gape.
Will the escaping ape escape?

I've been Here Sometime

I've been here sometime,
Living along, day to day,
Year to year, feeling and thinking,
Accepting and rejecting, loving and hating,
Positive and negative, completing the circuit
To let the power flow into glory.
Generally getting the hang of it all
While keeping my balance on, the often,
Thin edge of a moving metaphysic.

I've been here sometime
And am fully aware
Of the four elements of existence
And something of their subtle composition.
Though mostly it is
Of the rough experience
I have knowledge:
Of the earth; my lusts,
Of the fire; my passions,
Of the waters; my dreams,
And of the air; my visions.

I've been here sometime
And will repeat, I have knowledge;
Knowledge derived from a meditative stance
Effected to take the blows
Of a punch-drunk world.
I've been here sometime
And would repeat the years again,
Each second of time's assassination
So to be closer than I am
To how it really is,
To each hurt, each kiss,
To know better the living dimension.
I've been here sometime

And have no wish to leave
Now I am getting used to the place
And have taken some measure of its ways.
And, of course, I have earned my years.
The reward all strive for
With every day of living.
The skeleton in the cupboard
The young deny or shy from
Before they grow up to accept its heritage.

I've been here sometime
And long enough to know
However you escape
You are called back to the dark courts of life
Where justice and injustice are administered
By the magistracy of the self.

I repeat, I have knowledge.
The world my continent,
My country of belonging
I must conserve and cherish,
Hold balanced in the hand of my making,
Beautiful and healthy, to bear its fruit and its pleasure.

I walked the fields and the meadows
Kicking my heels amongst daisies,
Blowing my time on a blow clock,
Then followed my nose like a mongrel,
Untrained except for his senses,
After a distant, whining bitch on heat.
On the sweating beast of my terrors
I climbed to run blindly through brambles.
When clear I licked the blood of my scratches
To taste the hunger of the earth again.

And over and over, ineducable in schoolmaster's language,
Not learning my lesson they would say.

But I learned, the moral is unimportant,
Is like pain, a coward's deterrent
The poetry is over and over until the climax,
The coming, the orgasm, the contact with,
The knowledge that a happening is you.

I repeat I have knowledge.
In the earth my flesh, in my flesh the earth,
Fused together and breaking apart.
Animal and plant, elemental dust to dust,
Ashes to ashes. Nothing is lost
Only repeated, over and over, indestructible.

Here in my fifty-first year,
I ask the sun about rainbows,
Delight with the hills over valleys,
Listen to the gossip of grass,
Hear a fox bark, see a hawk swoop
And a tree shiver in the sun,
As though I walk in the world from the cradle:
For I have knowledge of wonder
To hold me here still and renew me
Over and over with its eternal revelations.

Fool's Testimony

Being I believe in my right fool's mind
I swear my truth on the new Spring leaf
And pen my faith with the gull's wings flying
Skywide, dream-deep over the sea of living.
I came jingling dreams in my pockets,
Gladly whistling my urchin tune,
Breaking and making my bastard heart,
Lashing the still waters to spume
As I sank in the depths of the part
Any fool, being the fool, forgets.
My only friends were the lonely
Sun and moon, my lover was she
In the rain weeping, the windy
Cry in the eaves and the pounding heart of the sea.

Nothing was mine that you gave me
For it was stamped with your seal.
You disowned me in your ordered world
Yet lashed me to your breaking wheel,
Garbed my innocence in guilt and hurled
My heart amongst your scrap to be
Melted down and made into a thing.
And now you charge me with the crime
Against the sane who daily bring
Their proud prisoners to the rope of time.

I plead not guilty! No crime I know
Other than the crime a fool commits
By stifling his true believing
With the curt 'choke collar' of his wits
Or from your Judas' lips receiving
The kiss that bruises like a blow.
All pains I know and none shall make
Me hold your mirror to my face;
My reflection's in the crystal lake,

My honour in the fool found grace.

And all that I possess is given
Tending the sullen seeds I've sown
In the thin soil between the day
To-day stones. Though bitter the wind's blown
In its season seed and soil away
And frost in the hope spring has bitten
My flowers to a fist of fingers,
Barked black and stiff stupid with toil,
One day shall come the harvest singers
Praising my flowers in fields they've made royal.

Hound Fool

I came limping over the lonely hill
Zigzagging my uncertain, certain way,
A hound fool crazed by an impelling scent,
Laid at some bitch time in my awakening brain.
Nothing had diverted me longer than to bay
Up at the fully summer-sated moon
And I stopped only when the trail appeared to end,
Because my nose failed to discern the scent
On the pissing run for every mongrel dog.
But past it I'll pick up the scent and go
Zigzagging my uncertain, certain way
I came limping over the lonely hill
To follow where it will not end.

Defeat – to a Man like Me

To a man like me,
Who admires courage above
All other killing things
That make life possible and whole,
What can I say
That is not cowardly and weak
When again I show
No courage to defeat
My first enemy?

The beast of fear
Beats me down at every move
I make to find escape
Past it to the wide,
Upright, shining light of pride;
Beats me down and makes me crawl
Back into the dark, sweating
Hovel of myself I make.

But when my enemy begins
To enter my dark hovel where
I thought it would not come
I crouch and watch it stumble
Unseeing in the dark and find
Its eyes are blind with light,
And I, the seer in the dark,
Can strike it to the heart
And leave it lying dead.
But when I reach the door
And open it to stride
Hero wise into the world of pride
I look but cannot see
The wide, upright, shining light
Of any victory.

The Odds

The secret's clear in every fable told
Of foolish rainbows with a pot of gold.
The chosen and unchosen thirst in line
Before the few are called and given wine.

I've seen the faces of a thousand men
Set to expected disappointment when
A time came to announce the lucky name,
For each one knew he had no right of claim.

And yet the one called out discovered how,
That moment, to accept. And on his face,
Smugly stupid as a sacred cow,
A look of inalienable right to grace.

That we believe our name is in the hat
Is why we stand so long in line or prayer.
The tricks we play, like any sewer rat,
Can only prove the odds and our despair.

Plea to Fate

I am a man, sir, like any other
Born to a mother
And raised with love to grow to my flower's shape,
Indistinguishable in the first spring crop,
With something of the nettle and the grape
In the over crowded fields of hop.

Why, sir, have you chosen me from all
To train against the wall,
Twisting my nature at your whim and will,
Torturing me with dreams I cannot know,
Keeping my roots in shallow soil to kill
The flowers that my green buds strive to grow?

What is it, sir, that makes you want to keep
Me bound so I'll not reap
The little harvest that for so hard I've striven?
It cannot be you think I'll not abide
By the boundaries that you have given
In your law. Could it be your sense of pride?

Even so, sir, I still don't understand
Or am I, on your land,
Something that you hadn't planned to grow this time?
Is your planning so obdurate that I,
Unlike the many, commit a crime
For which all my envisaged flowers must die?

Please, sir, I only ask you'll let me be
That which I am and free
To put out new shoots that you'll not cut,
Disfigure, maim or trample on with scorn.
I can take my chance and hope for luck, but
To resist your willing I was not born.

On a Morning Such as This

On a morning such as this
with the sky wide open for light
and the air cool with speeches to stir
the dew-kissed lovers from sleep
I send the dog out first to die,
discretion being my part to play
while a dead hero
has no status at the corner shop,
romanticism being no longer valid
as a ticket for a free meal.
So I send the dog out first
then smell warily around the door
thinking hard on the facts of life,
taking a fag like an antidote.
This way I'm hardly ever surprised.
If the singing birds betray me
I curse them for a bloody row
setting my mind off on the left foot,
killing my robin.
Then, smearing the little blood like a badge
of courage for cynicism
and armoured up ready for any blow
from the worldly day,
I go out to meet my mis-appointments.

Now We Must Begin Again

Now we must begin again
The incredible journey.
Too long we have rested,
Dallying with girls and drinking
Sweet wine from old bottles.
We have told all our stories
And repeated our lies over and over
Until they've almost become
Our truth. Although we know
Only the journey is true
And real the road we must travel.

Yes, there is comfort here
And lulled to contentment
We put off our preparations
To resume our journey;
Each day saying, 'tomorrow,
Tomorrow we shall start'.
But tomorrow we wake late
Or forget, caught in the trap
Of trivialities.
And we let the womens' eyes lead us
Where their hands hold still our hearts.

And tenderly they can break us to
Rising from their beds one morning
To find the way across the mountains
Lost in mists, the winter come,
The vision that once lured us on
A ghost to haunt us at a fearful time
And our empty children destined to say,
'We have nowhere to go
For you have lost the way'.

Look! The Sun has set again,
The evening dusk creeps in.

The women smile contentedly
And we feel the little wind blow by
Waving the tops of trees.
Our children watch us curiously
Almost as though they know
Our need has not the will to go
And we avoid their eyes and turn
Our backs, busying ourselves until
Darkness and the road are one.

The Believers

Out of your regret shall spring rainbows
And as grass grows so shall you forget,
With your laughter rivers burst their banks
To flood with your thanks the fields after
The dry season.
For no reason
Of Spring there shall come buds to dead wood
And as good as gold to the dumb
Your song will sing, and your heart absurd
Will believe the word your love shall bring.

From your despair down you shall tumble,
Proud to be humble as the trees bare.
You will give praise though your hour to live
Shall come just to give minutes to days
In the long time.
Though you shall climb
To the stars on hope forged in hell fire
You will go higher. Though we must grope
In the dark lie the way is for you
A vision passed through the needle's eye.

Part II: Love Poems

Life

Life's like the springing step of youth.
Life's like an aching rotten tooth.
Life smoulders on for years
Like wet grass dampened by fire
Until suddenly love kicks it bright
To flare and dance with hot delight
To life's conflagration of desire.

I've Always Loved Women

I have always loved women,
My trousers up or down.
And not just the common
Suckling, feeding of renown,
Dutifully loving Mums,
Or wives, family chums
But as I love a poem,
A piece of music or
The unattainable.
In the cinema, aged eight,
The girl who slapped my face
Held tightly to my hand.
An understanding grace
That men all fail to state
Except in words too grand.
I've always loved women,
And will.

Sun and Rain

Rain runs softly down gutters
And the sun shines again
Polishing the mirrors of puddles
With its golden vanity.
The smell of the bright, washed air
Is of a women from her wash-day kitchen.

I remember how you looked
Coming from your wash-day kitchen
To answer my knock when I called.
Your face was flushed and damp,
Your hair untidy and the smell of you
Was of warm air washed by summer rain.

I look at the sky, blue with your eyes blue,
Watch the hung out sheets of clouds
Billowing before the wind
And smell your warm body as this air,
So the world becomes you through all
My five senses to behold.

A man jostles me, passing by,
And I turn, startled to see
People smiling at me as they stare.
Perhaps the sun and rain has blessed them too
With visions of a love.

A Little Loving

'D'you want a little loving, honey?'
Her voice was soft her eyes unseen.
I said, 'I haven't got that money.'
She laughed, believing me between
The possibility and why,
Laughing easily as birds fly.

I stopped, condemned by eyes of one
Who brushed me by with living clean.
A little loving? I had none.
She smiled. God knows I had not seen
A woman smile me favour for
So long and she was called a whore.

A little loving. She was young,
With no pretence and would not care
That all my dreams had not been sung.
And with her I could even dare
To laugh, think happiness, be kind
And forget enough to make me blind.

A little loving? All I'd earned
In forty years of dying came
To just the little loving yearned,
To be accepted without shame
Or show. Her mouth was like a flower
That would die, for me, within the hour.

I Love You

Of course it's easy to say, I love you.
A cliche turned on the lathe of my tongue
As in any other word factory.
Common as dandruff on sloping shoulders,
Grey as yesterday's screwed up newspaper,
Tasteless as bread without any butter.
I love you, I love you, I love you is passion
As second hand as news on the Telly.
Then what can I say to my woman
For her to know, first hand, my feelings?
Only can I say, you fulfil me,
Raise me, breathe on my fossil to give me
Life, pleasure and pain to make me known
Famous to myself in the praises of my blood.
You're the author of the song of myself
That I sing above the roar of the city
And the daily inconsequence of actions.
So I climb the mountain of my self esteem
Singing to call my Ishmael from the desert.
And yet such high flown words only stretch
The same old love sprung language
To where it loses recoil and goes limp.
Then what can I say to you, my dear,
More than another million lovers?
I'll say the same old love worn cliche,
I love you, imitative as each year's Spring
But new and unsullied as though there was never
Spring before in the sequence of seasons.

And Began

The beginning a casual start.
Hardly more than a wink your eye.
Quick smile, turn away and –

A day falls, a rain drop
On a wet afternoon of eternity.
A black cloud frowns from the heavens.
A woman cries out for a man
Brimming with brimstone love.
I walked through the streets of the raindrop
Clutching my heaven in the hard fists of my heart.
Hardly noticing the drooped moustache look
Of the beer town, barmaid's apron smelling.
Around the buttocks of the Trent valley.

Of course a beginning is indicative
But of what? Is the sperm, egg, foetus
Indicative of – except to pre-knowledge?
What then is beginning.
The first thought, word or incident that happens
Seed sown, bud, explosion of blossom
Filling the belly of Spring
To a pregnant Summer?
How can a beginning begin without goal?
I saw her that evening and the seed was set.
That was the beginning, the coming together
The law of gravitation, atmospheric pressure
Never astound us, having always been.
So it was a casual start.
All the facts were known,
There was no groping about in a dark room
For a secret panel hiding a possible treasure.
The room was lit, the panel open
And the treasure there.
We were concerned with what the treasure could buy,
And we bought the world
Paying in cash there and then without quibble;
And began.

Two Poems for Her

Of course, my dear, he would be so kind,
The sports-car youth whose name had slipped your mind.
There are many such who'd take you out and numb
Your passion with their schoolboy's love and then
Blushing happily take you home to Mum.
A nicely normal and forever end.

And no doubt, my dear, there are many men
Handsome, clever, rich and free and ten
Times my worth in all that's considered good
Who'd fondly make you their enchanting wife;
But I can give you nothing but the rod
And staff and gasping miracle of life.

I run my fingers through your hair,
Night sung, soft and summer breezes,
Stroke your temples, waters where
The moon refracts its treasured secrets.
My mouth with all its human lies
I dare not trust to tell the stars,
That light the spring dark of your eyes,
Of my tender, aching love that swears
Its truth in oaths of flesh and lust.
But when for you my flesh is dust
The summer breezes through your hair
Shall be my loving fingers there.

After She has Left

I close my book, stub my cigarette
Then slowly push my shoe off with my foot,
Take off the other shoe by hand and walk
As in some holy penance, in my socks
Through to the kitchen and gaze around.
I open the pantry but feel no need.
I pick up an apple and put it down,
Temptation tasteless as though my flesh
Had been neutered in the blood and cell.
I go to the bathroom, clean my teeth,
Wind my watch, a day ending now
Meaningless as any hour is to a clock.
I slowly get undressed and lowly see
My shrunken shadow ugly on the wall
And freeze anger in my bitterness to call
My pride formally to explain
In cold, precise sentences the dream.
I climb in the coffin of my bed,
Switch off the light to the darkness tomb
And lie unthinking in the senseless blank
Of blackness that envelopes all.
But living still my animal scents your smell
On the pillow where your sweet head lay
And the grass is fresh and green with dew
And warm the sunshine from the Spring of you.

I Run a Sweet Risk

I run a sweet risk
My neck in the noose of love
But what else for a capital gain
When a man lives
By the blood in his veins.

And my blood runs warmer,
Faster, clearing the old, sour
Jaundice, yellowing a young despair,
Stretching my heart to hold
Visions my youth was too green to bear.

Eye for an eye, heart for a heart
Reward and punishment shocks
The smooth complacency that clogs
With sentimentality. The blood beats
Vibrating the amoeba flesh
To life beyond death.

I run a sweet risk
My neck in the noose of love
But no other way
Can I die so I can live.

Only Possible

I waited one cold evening outside where,
Not over much enamoured with the world.
Waited and saw the crowds go by
Unpunished and unpleasured by it all.
Waited with small impatience for I knew
You would come, though late, would come to me.
Then I'd understand why rivers flow, winds blow,
Sun shines and all the foolish crowds go by.
For me to make meaning out of life and accept it so
Is only possible through the alchemy of you.

For my Private Keeping

Casually I came, with casual thoughts
Thinking of coffee or just her warming room.
Began to chat of poetry and projects,
Lit her cigarette and stole again
The colour of her eyes for my private keeping
And saw the darkened hollows beneath her eyes
Still taut from weeping.
She said, 'A trivial thing,
A little stupid quarrel' and talked a little,
Laughed again and felt, she said,
'Much better' in less than half an hour.
I treasure now her sadness and her pleasure
And when I light her cigarette in future
Shall look and take the beauty of her eyes
For my private keeping
As a gift naturally and sincerely given.

After I Phoned You

Lonely? Not really,
Though I miss you
Like an amputee a limb,
Or an answer
To an unanswerable question,
Which is, perhaps, the only thought for love.
Not lonely because you are always
My blessing,
The light in my head,
The get through the day feeling
Of better things to come.
Lonely is to be without the question.
Lonely? I shall not be
While you remain with me.

When You Leave Me

I am a grown man, not afraid
Though wise enough to be
Respectful of the dark.
I keep a somewhat jaundiced eye
On the seductive stars,
Put change straight into my pocket without counting,
Have risked my neck a time or two,
Survived my fright and believe
In God, mostly
Because humanists are so pompous
And their morality pathetic
And humans, thank God, are human.

I am a man, man enough to question
Myself and find approximate answers,
Man enough to forgive, after my anger,
All the hurts that heal over.
Man enough to be selfish and unselfish,
Man enough to know
Love is more that I can master,
Above all man enough to show
I am man enough to accept love's domination.

So? I have boasted and unboasted my claim
To manhood. But hear me!
I am afraid, afraid when you leave me.
I am empty as a untenanted house
With unfurnished rooms and bare floors
To walk on, unlit and unheated.
I am afraid and lonely,
An unmade man, a completed jigsaw
Jumbled into pieces to await
Your return and be reassembled to a picture.

I am nothing, a vacuum, non-existent,
A shadow that the going down of your sun
Eliminates.

When you leave me believe in me or I
Shall never be again or could ever have existed.

I Will Not Terrify the Hour

I will not terrify the hour
With any thought to violate
The contemplation of tall trees
On windless evenings after rain,
The facts I know like any child
And yet, as he will keep them shut
Behind strong doors that only I
Can open to destroy and maim.
The beautiful is calm, relaxed,
I rest my head against her breast
And listen to her beating heart
Sound clear each syllable of love,

Death is murder and panic breaks
The evolution of the hour,
Every walker on the waters
Prepares his miracle within
That calm centre of belief
Where fool and wise man learn alike
The inevitability of life.
So I shall not disrupt this hour
With any thought of pain or death.
The tortured and the dead can claim
Their brother only in their name.

Glass Dream

Supposing I saw her now
After these fifteen thinking years,
Saw her, O God, somehow
In this mockery of no tears?

Supposing I knew her still,
As lovely as I dreamed before,
What failure in my will
Could have betrayed the oath I swore?

Supposing some watchless day,
In a lull between thought and thought,
Eyes meeting mine should say,
I'm really the truth you've sought?

Supposing? But thoughts like stones
Come shattering the dreams of glass.
Cold are the fleshless bones,
And the visions are ghosts that pass.

Depression

The air is still and oppressive,
Making breathing a conscious effort.
Noises in the street are overdone,
Like bad theatre and the rain,
That threatened all day long,
Holds off as though denying
Absolution.

I lie with myself, a stranger,
For you're not here to give me joy
With hands and body to destroy
Through long moments all my anger.

Midnight and tomorrow broods upon its future.
A ship trumpets across the harbour
Like a bull elephant calling to its cow.
But its majesty calls without answer
And the silence closes over, except
For the nibbling noises of non-entities.
I lie and listen, listen till I fall asleep
To awake in the morning
With nothing changed by the light.

Even If

Even if we go
Back to where we know our love was meant,
With the scent of jasmine to provoke
All that we spoke of love,
And unglove our tender dreams
From the protection of the years
Only tears will flow.

Even if we make,
Out of heartbreak, snowdrops with no Spring
Who will sing away the thoughts that learn,
On the turn of hope, despair?
And shall we wear the blossom
To a joy on clothes worn old
Or hold in arms ache?

Even if we could,
Out of dead wood, fashion something green
Wouldn't our lean jealousies devour
The first flower? And hearing the cry
Of wild birds high above the marsh
Would we not shoot then down to bless
A mess of flesh and blood?

Even if we find
New ways to be kind we shall be cruel
Testing the jewel for flaws and unable
In the fable to believe
We shall conceive a clever tale
To open wide our eves to see
Less than the truly blind.

The Widower

After slowly putting his bike in the shed
He closed the door and followed where the path led
Towards the house, bent down to see the blight
On potato leaves in the fading light,
Then, wiping his shoes, entered the cold house.
He switched on the light and watched it dowse
The dozing darkness from kitchen shelves
But ignored the mirror of his passing selves.
He removed his coat, put away his shoes,
Switched on the wireless, heard the aching news
And waited until the whistling kettle boiled
Slumped in his shirt that had its collar soiled.
So he made the tea, one teaspoonful only,
Poured and sat drinking it as the lonely
Clock sipped seconds from time's unemptying cup.
He watched through the window the moon come up,
Wrote on the dusty dresser his finger mark
And listened for her from the sobbing dark.

Love poems Part 2: Poems to Vera

Affidavit

Content as country butter and serene
As waters guarded round by mountains are
All day in sunshine and untroubled air.
At night to draw the cold stars down
And embracing warm them to reflect
Their silver into streams of golden light.
I see her happiness like this and cry
My gods of beauty and of truth down to
Be witness to this affidavit sworn
In my name of poet and man
To keep her happiness inviolate
From the cold and bitter winds my climate blows.

Portsmouth Harbour 8.45 p.m. 7th July 1971

A note to Vera

It is cool now, with a slight breeze
Rippling the water,
I bring beer from the 'Lone Yachtman'
And sit on a bench with your absence
As my companion.
I know you will be happy here
And that thought calms me
So I am content to look
And take my fix on the future.
The sun goes down on the Solent,
A golden submarine submerging
To leave its wake trembling
In a path to another world
That could tempt a tourist dreamer
To walk his miracle across.
Faintly, beautiful in the distance,
A sad bugle sounds
To the lowering of flags:
An old sailor remembers
And spits the lump in his throat
Into the dark gathering water.
The sun completes its stately descent
And the blushing complimented sky
Fades slowly to twilight to beckon stars.
I finish my beer watching a small cruiser
Sail on a light breeze towards a calm sea.

Eight More Days

Another day, another year to wait
I light another cigarette and stare
Through the window at my guests of sparrows
Who gobble scattered breadcrumbs in the snow,
Jubilantly suspicious of free meals.
The winter sunshine smiles a consolation prize.
I pace about the room and count the days.
Eight more days, a week not counting this day now.
So many weeks I've lost and can't recall,
Forgotten in some blessed amnesia.
So will another week be such a loss?
I sit, light a cigarette and watch the smoke
I blow in rings; tossing sighs into
A lake of air. Your breasts are rounder,
Firmer, soft as snow and warm against my mouth.
In the garden sparrows peck at breadcrumbs
With such frenzy for they know such gifts are rare.
I press my forehead hot against the window pane.
Tenderer your caressing fingers soothed.
Eight days, a week's eternity to lose.
Hell's sweat behind a shovel twenty years
Was easier than these years of twenty days.
I kissed your mouth and love flowed sweet
To quench the thirst of all those dried out years.
I touched your body and healed all my wounds and hurt.
Your arms close round me and I sigh content.
Another week? I could leap a thousand years,
For you'll be there to catch and take my hand.
Eight days, seven, not counting this day now,
I'll shake out of my mind, as sparrows must
Their hunger when a frozen morning ends
In a gift of breadcrumbs fit for banqueting,
These twenty frozen days, when you return to me.
But if one time my arms tighten till they hurt,
Or I bite till pleasure feels its pain,
Forgive me, I shall be only shutting out the thought
Of this separation, and fear of you going away again.

One Autumn

I dropped the phone and left the box,
Saw asphalt sky and dying trees,
The patched fields darned with grey sheep flocks
The rain like cold sweats of disease,

Passed little houses made of stones
Each with its joyless coffin bed,
Heard the dirge from wires of phones
Calling the numbers of the dead.

I watched the withered hearts of leaves
Falling to their rotting place
Yet still my stupid heart believes
I'll know the summer of your grace.

And All That I shall Ever Write

And all that I shall ever write,
Before the morning, beyond the night,
Could not whisper and could not shout
Softer, louder what life's about
Than my dumb lips on your dumb lips
Or our silent speaking finger tips.
O never be it otherwise!
The gift line is given in our eyes
And lips and hands and bodies make
The sleeping poetry come awake
To sing and celebrate above
Our mean knowledge and poor love.

I Fool

I fool around god
Buddha-like dove held
In a hand frightened with love
Searching the dark cave
Sobbing a name no
One has crucified with fame.

Answer and answer
Darkness with light of
The vision that shatters sight
For I fool can hear
Your heart death beating
Singing soft as child's breath.

Finding you I fool
Buddha-like dove held
In a hand frightened with love
And gasp the eternal
Moment of making
Out in a poem for your sake.

To Be Continued

To Vera

I

Love can simply be said to lie
With the making and the mating.
Or, in the colloquialism of cocks and cunts,
Arguing the toss of loving, hating,
Of course the fundamentals are inherent here,
The bare necessities and the savage aching,
The reciprocity of giving, taking;
Pleasure trespassing on pain, joy's forbidden.
Marked by frontier cries like fear and panic
And the holding on, O save me,
Enslave me, time stop and pleasure drain me.

II

Let me begin again.
In the beginning, before the quickened heart beats,
The eyes half signalling, the hands reaching
In the mind but unmoving, undaring to touch,
Beautiful is the vulnerability of humans,
Before this the man, the woman is
Present to each other in the sense of radar,
Or of a dimension known to migrating birds,
At a time, a season unquestionable as birth.
As in a poet a poem's gestation quickens to be known,
Or in a woman's breasts a faint tingling hails
A life conceived before the seed is fully set.
Aware of the presence of each other,
Two grains of sand in the desert of the human race.
So miracles are possible, like this.
And before the miracle is made manifest
What luck or cunning, design or gift
Moved the elements to shift in ways
That two grains of man could join
Together and fulfil a miracle, a love

That is. And being now was once conceived
In some rapture prophesying the moment of our sense
That we who need beginnings call the miracle of birth.

III

Spring will out.
Laughter is not impossible at the gravest times.
I have it on the authority of wonder,
In the blessing of the blood's evangelist
In the high pulpit and on the silent source of song
That love's despite
The anger of angels, alienation from the garden,
The catastrophe of continents and our
Own infidel doubt.

IV

We walked in the dark place, a past recalling,
Conscious of its ending.
I waited, patient with impatience,
Knowing you would say my question.
'What is the tower I've seen?'
A tower of magic. You knew the answer,
As I, had read the fable
In our eyes of children.
We climbed to the top of the tower
Only speaking the words of places and things.
Yet between the thought of separation
And our case-hardened realities
We used the wavelength of love's dimension
To ask questions and give answers
And communicate our decision in a moment
Of towered magic high above Leicestershire.

Being a part *(for Vera)*

You will return,
Your eyes full of Rubens, the line
Of a river, charm of a street,
New faces and places I have not seen.

You'll not be sure
If the pictures you saw, a face
During dinner, on river, or street
Flashed you a smile that must dim my conceit.

So will your ears
Hear sounds I am deaf to, recall
Evening laughter, talk in a bar,
A music engendered from being apart.

Strange you will feel
Seeing me different, your smile
As before, but apprehensive,
Your sweet hands touching, perhaps, not sure.

Being a part
Is always for ever.

Strange *(for Vera)*

Do you remember how your father stood,
Distant as winter trees through window glass
And you alone in the heated room admired?
Often you look at me and smile to find
The windows of that overheated room are wide
And those trees are near and leafed in full.
Strange how a little girl could wish so much
And set the truth of needed love aright.

For Vera on Her Eightieth Birthday

She's clever, witty with more stories that
The whole Arabian Nights,
Boccaccio and Canterbury man.
She's a woman who still charms, delights
Not some eighty year old alsoran
But woman given those insights
That only brave survival can.
Loved by many as are her rights
But more by this most lucky man.

And Forever

(for Vera)

I bring you flowers to display
My love,
So you can look at them and say
Above
All else he has remembered me,
Carried in his head my reality.
So turn
And smile at me so I will see
Your love,
Through all these years, returned to me.

Part III: Blades of Grass

At Horsley Lake

I watch the ducks
Walking like fat women
And wonder at the echoes down the years
Of the language of things,
The lake still with no wind
And the dreaming trees in the water,
A fisherman casting his line
Contemplating the navel of nature
And the water lilies on their beds of leaves
Dozing in the afternoon sun.
An aeroplane leaving or entering Gatwick
Is no more than an empty thought
Crossing the mind and forgotten.
The breathing peace of the place
Slows the blood in the veins
Quietening the mind like a kindness
Given by a passing stranger.
No miracle this but an offering
In this country of England.

A Quiet Evening

A quiet evening falls
Across a sunset sky.
The sun no longer burns
And yet its passions stay
Warm at the close of day.

The colours of the flowers
Fade with twilight hours
And yet their forms and scents
Create a haunting innocence.

The majestic Atlas trees
Hold up a lover's heaven
As the moon rises up to give
All lovers a kindly light
So the plainest lover feels
Blessed and beautiful.

Seascape

A pageant of porpoises, a circus of delight,
Masters of their world man never attained.
A trawler trailing a bridal train of gulls,
A ballet of birds wheeling on the wind
Mocking the clumsiness of planes
And diving gannets flashing into the sea
Of rich diamonds mined by the sun.
O Mozart did even you
Make magic to so enchant.

Tranquility

The sky is close, the streams run slow,
A tree with knowledge droops its head,
The grass is silent, all's been said;
The fields past moody hedgerows flow
With timeless patience into space
And nothing, nothing's out of place.

O how peaceful the world is now
After yesterday and before
Tomorrow and its threatening year!
That gliding bird, that grazing cow
Will glide and graze for evermore
And everything we know be clear.

Sea Call

I look at the sea
And feel its great immensity
Its wild surging of desire
To overwhelm the earth
And take us back to our beginnings.
Its constant ebb and flow
Is heard in the rhythms of music
And in the gasp and sigh of our breath.
We taste it in the salt of our blood,
In the tears of joy or sorrow.
In our loving juices flow
The sea's unfathomable mystery.
I listen and hear it speak
Deep in the throat of time,
Crying, calling me back
To the drowning darkness of its depths
To know the first and only miracle.
But the gulls scream, beware, beware!
And I step back to the safe land
And take a pebble in my hand
To grasp its solid certainty.

By the River

River bank, heron and curlew
Willows whispering to the water
On the breath of the breeze
Secrets only the fishes know.
I sit and wonder watching the river flow
As placidly as passing time
This peaceful Sunday afternoon,
A canoe glides by quiet
As a basking crocodile.
A tree sighs sleepily,
A leaf falls, treading the air
Lighter than a ballet dancer,
Spins a pirouette
And touches the water gently
Like a farewell kiss.
The reeds sway as a choir
Of children singing a favourite hymn.
I watch and listen, recording
This summer afternoon in my album of memories
To take out and lighten a darker day.

Unfinished Song

In this coupling summer, poised
Cavalier on the edge of winter,
Flowers flaunt their colours, brave
Protests in the face of powers
That rage to crush them into grey.
The days are shining shields to hang
In the golden armoury of the sun,
Each with its heroic fable sung
Lovely on the evening air with stars.

Near a Bridge at Henley-on-Thames

I sit and watch the water
River by, untroubled and uncaring
Only knowing that it can flow.
A bird freeways across the sky
And the sun shines its blessing.
Trees mirrored in the water
Shimmer with delight
At their own image.
A swan glides by, royal
As Cleopatra's barge.
I hear the traffic roaring over the bridge
Like an invading army
From an alien world,
But I feel unthreatened
Cocooned in this ambience
Of pleasantness and charm.
This I need like a nourishment
To feed me and sustain me
In this modern world's reality.

Listening to a Song

Out of the song the words ghost
Into that shut door room of my mind,
Tracing cobwebs of pain
With skinny fingered love.
A dark corner flashes with a smile
To blind my eyes with seeing.
Regret forms in my veins like ice
Cooling the warm life of my love.

Sad it is that the past
Falls like leaves to rot;
And yet the loam laid down
Feeds this summer's leaves and flowers.
But those ghosts are always there
As sea breezes on summer evenings
Are cold on skin burning with a full day's sun.
Only the paler shadows fall
On nights millionaired with stars.

The Mountains

Viewed from a distance, dreamy lumps,
Heaps poured from the great blue bucket of the sky.
We began to climb. A path, a promenade to walk.
Two hours walking and still the mountain grew;
Closer but remoter, withdrawn and brooding
On the intensity of its mass. With colder eyes
It looked on us. Drew us up
To chill our bodies and our minds and stop
The flow of blood of our belief to iron
And granite in our veins of hope,
And so to crush and overpower us and make
Us prisoners in the great vaulted dungeon
Of compressed immensity.
It would make us of the stone and mountain air,
Contract, shrivel and capture us
To belong forever and renounce our claim
To the freedom of our weakness and our domain
Of fallibility.
Still we climbed on, up the steeper compulsive ways,
And came to a frozen, imprisoned lake,
Guarded in its tomb by eunuch peaks
Against the warm, running life escape.
We stopped and gazed upon the icy face
And heard the choirs of silence gathered there
Singing an everlasting requiem.

Death is not sudden, coming as surprise
But is constant, present in the dream of things,
Relevant in the context of our minds,
Communicating with mountains and with seas.
We were not ready, with a life to make
Before the time when we would dare mistake
A frontier so defined and venture past.
Like wild beast or humble sheep we know

Such lines are drawn by our own frailty.
So we keep strictly to our side or on the line
Sleep, unthink, pretend or take gods' hands
And awake far from our anxiety.

On the lower, controllable slopes of man
The sun shone and we again exclaimed,
How beautiful! Walked light of step,
Saw the mountain high above us reign
Over our projected sense of majesty.
So, warm and reassured, we swung along,
Glanced at the lower slopes littered with rocks
And likened them to fallen men in battles
Fought in some history we could not call our own.
We reached our car, relieved and drove away
Talking happily and gay of many things
And felt the mountain shrink behind our speed
And us grow up into ourselves again
Proud humans who could release the frozen lake,
Conquer any mountain and unhear awhile
The requiem of silence that sings so near.

Sonnet April 93

O randy spring let the sap rise and flow
And we'll not court the origin of sin
Now new found warmth persuades the heart to glow.
How cheekily the hedgerows greenly grin
As children skip and run without their coats
And people smile at strangers on the street.
Amateur sailors launch their sailing boats
While somehow aches and pains deny defeat.
Let all of us, we're nature's creatures too,
Shout and sing in our individual way,
Bring forth those flowers that modern fashions rue.
Gaining tomorrow what is scorned today.
The enjoyment of ordinary things
Is a miracle man's perception brings.

Hot Day, No Sun (N.W.II)

Hot day, no sun,
Thunder and rain will come.
Garden ghettos, avenues,
Close as dung flies on their heap,
Noise of traffic sweating out
The surplus of a fat despair.
Who am I to wander here
Alien as an arab in
The unholy and unpromised land.
A sparrow on the potted lawn
Pecks the prepacked decadence
Unknowing or uncaring how
Tomorrow is not like today –
Or that givers go away.
Hot day, no sun,
Thunder and rain will come.

Entry in a Late Summer Diary

The warm, dry weather persists.
The trees look languid with too much summer love
And the streams stroll slowly
Singing their troubadour sad songs.
Here and there a few leaves fall,
Omens of the dying that's to come.
Escapist birds prepare for ritual journeyings
And anxious realists sniff prematurely the Winter's spoor.
Today, tomorrow, perhaps another month
This summer will hold its heaven high.
I neither prepare nor sniff its ending near;
Perhaps afraid, but who cares what you say.
I now know how the seasons run,
Have caught on to the simple two and two
Of living where night must follow day
And would be less human if I weren't afraid.
And today the sky is unclouded and the last hay
As sweet to lie in as anything in May.

Believing

It's all believing
In the wide eyed light,
The world possible and revealing,
All that we knew come right.
Even us belonging
In the simple falling
Of things into place
With the calling of birds
And the forming
Of trees in their grace;
When the sun, saviour and shining,
Haloes over the hill
In the true majesty of rising
With such triumph to fill
The earth and the worm with glory.

With the unfolding of flowers
And the leaves green and lovely
The smiling of the windows of houses
Reflecting happiness as humble
As the goodness of summer laughing
With its freedom of being reborn.
This is us seeing
With the faith of our eyes
With the belief of our ears hearing
And how our hearts decree
It must be for our sakes, dreaming
Out of our minds a vision,
Ultimate and compelling
With the power of praise.

The Fallen Season

Now, in this fallen season,
With summer gone and winter yet to come
The gunboat threatening skies
Compromise with rain,
Winds blow no flutes of guttering
To a dance of falling leaves.
The little houses sit and stare
At their image across the street
Bored all evening up to bed.
Mock lovers hurriedly unknow,
In bleak bus shelters or cornered dark,
Their contraceptive love and sow
No sacred seeds of innocence.
The raincoat weary figures walk
Towards the queue of evening hours,
Knowing the rations they will get
Will keep them only just alive
And all the promises they heard
From demagogues of blood and heart
Were never possible or died
On warm and laughing summer lips.

Autumn Evening

Autumn evening into night
Fading noises; fading light;
How the lowly sun has burned
Into cinders those green hills
That beckoned so before life turned
The corner where all wonder spills
Its sweet water into sand.

Inhumanities at hand
Make sour cynics of us all;
And childhood flowers turn to dust.
All the songs that we recall
Have sentiments we distrust.
Does the sun of beauty cast
Rays of light where none can bask?

Winter Trees

Stripped of their vocabulary of leaves
The trees, like deaf mutes, stand accused,
Their glory and their pride abused
By sneers of the demagogic wind.
Their summer triumph's in defeat
Mocked by the traitorous rain's sharp sleet.
Yet still they are princes of the field
And though the sovereign sun they praise
Dies in high dungeons of winter days
They strike the sky with their dark salute.

Storm Wind

Suddenly the air awakes,
Stretches, yawns,
Shakes the hibernating grass,
Hesitates,
Gathers up its power and flies,
Starts the racing of the skies.

Winter trees, well reefed down,
Wave their spars
Like well-anchored sailing boats.
Stronger gusts,
Rattling windows, doors and fence,
Scream hymns of malevolence.

Rushing like a maddened crowd,
Throats roaring
Blasphemies to call up hate
And destroy
In a final tearing spasm;
A terrible orgasm.

Though Winter Comes

Of course it's finished now,
Summer being the shortest season.
And love leaks like a punctured tyre,
Slow or fast, which ever way
Goes flat and can't be ridden on
To escape.
The wound of winter begins to ache,
Exploratory doubts finger it with fear
And we cuddle up to care,
Fastidious nurse, possessive shrew,
And hang our loves, like still life,
In the museums of our minds,
To be viewed with the right detachment
And the Freudian comment
In spare moments from
Our full time occupation of the self.
And so we settle in,
Well stocked up with cliches to condone the first
Cold strike.
Composed and cheerful as
The sexless afternoon of sunday time
Begins, resigned in slippers and
Handy about our little house
To pass for purpose, though purpose be
Existence only to experience
The impossible, audacious day
When the whore of Spring comes laughing in.

Blades of Grass

In this prison land on a dirge of river
Their old lag's ambivalence
Is slop sided to a need to accept,
Circumstances being inescapable
In a complex labyrinth of losing.
O they shake the bars,
Raise the fists of their laughter,
Threatening the sane warder
And weep in their corner like a lullaby
Till sleep comes with the succubus of dreams.
But knowingly they grin
When the walker in the meadow drags his feet,
Treading down the flowers with the blades of grass
Indiscriminately.
For mostly the flowers break and wither
But the grass is more resilient,
Taking its hurt untragically
To sing again on the wind.

When Mankind Is Dead

When mankind is dead
Will there remain some sign
That we were here at all;
A stain on the rocks,
An echo of a scream
Carried on the wind
For a new life to fear
That we might return?
Will the trees remember in their roots
How we destroyed their forests,
And the air still taste our tainted breath?
Will the earth, polluted by our graves,
Germinate the seeds no more;
Could all the seas ever wash away
The world's grief?

Enlightenment

And the sun shone.
And the trees nodded the afternoon away,
Sleepy with the warm, wine air;
Like tolerant patriarchs,
Hardly disturbed by the comings and goings
Of the fussing infants of birds.
And the grasses scratched each other's backs
And whispered wisely over their common gossip.
While the daisies, like children dressed
For an old fashioned Sunday occasion
Held their heads high for smiling
And a distant rabbit danced no shadows
Falling of snares and foxes.
Only my feet, brushing through meadow,
Released the 'blow clocks' into drifting,
Musing their dream-like, 'she loves me'
Song and dance of a fable storied away.
So for the moment I was the sun shining,
A blade of grass, tree dreaming
And warm, belonging and knowing the clay,
Air and all, because
I accepted them, with myself, as being.
And lying down in the long grass
Broke the fever of my fears
And I slept to the lullaby of midges
And awoke, like falling in love, to the world.'

A Sparrow at My Table

A sparrow flew to my table
At a city pavement cafe.
He was dressed in work-a-day feathers
And he nodded as though greeting
An old acquaintance, not a stranger.
Hopping on Olive Oyl legs
He was a street entertainer
Chirp, chirp song and dance performer
And all for the crumbs of my scone.
I loved his cheeky bravado
As he pecked the food from my plate.
Away he flew like a blessing
I'd welcome at each morning break,
For I felt honoured and chosen
As I walked away in delight.

Part IV: Memories

Memories of Childhood

After I turned the brooding corner,
Between the ranks of hard faced houses
With their steely polished windows
Staring cold pride across the street,
I became a fearless rebel
Stamping loudly with defiant feet,
Challenging the doorway shadows
Hump-backed with their burdens of guilt.

Beyond the town I sauntered,
Climbed the tower at the harbour's mouth
To gaze beyond a child's horizon
Like a prisoner in a foreign land.
There the calling sea I answered
With daydreams of sailing south
In a pirate ship with Morgan
Steered by my midshipman's hand.

From tower to beach I scrambled
My shoes grumbling the stones like parents
Quarrelling in a distant room.
Then listening to the waves repeating
Their high hopes and disillusion
In the undertow's deepward gasp
I sat down and quietly wondered
As the cool sea breeze of evening
Blew through my thin summer shirt.

Afternoon Note

I sit at the top of the Round Tower,
The sun on my face and the sea breeze salting my pleasure.
I watch the winged boats sailing across the Solent
Bent to their tasks like athletes,
For all the prizes of dreams.

This is my home now, there, just across the harbour,
In a small house, in a narrow street,
Comfortable as a cockle in its shell;
A Spring tide's ebb from the water.

It's five years since I emerged
From a hole in the ground in the Midlands,
Blinking into the light of my future.
Yet only now, in this given hour,
Is the celebration.

A man can have too little or too much.
Equally they are anathema.

I balance in my fifty third year,
With the ease of a new experience,
Between having and not having
Too much or too little.
Not envious or guilty I'm able
To idle the afternoon away
Quietly with my air and sea friends
Though fully conscious of the eyes on my back.

Those Days

My memory returns to those days
Of unencumbered youth
And such surety of life,
Those motorcycle years.
The speed, the thrill, the ton-up-boys.
The girl on the pillion
With thighs open wide,
Her arms round my waist
Holding tight to certainty.
The fallings off and near misses
The adolescent kisses
And the fumblings towards manhood
Realised in nineteen thirty nine
With volunteering to disappointment.

City Bus Ride

We rode high,
Doubledeckering into the city,
Whipping past streets lined with dormitoried cars
And a few soiled shops huddled like hurting,
The houses deaf mutes to the hurrying noise.
Then slowing hesitantly we entered the presence
Of the tall buildings, aloof in their dignity,
Where traffic lights were beckoning and stopping
Our bus, its engine throbbing like an anxious heart,
Then jerking forward, a polite giant, edging slowly
Into the frantic shuffling of cars
Surrounded with new shops, guilty with brightness,
Our bus stopped and we alighted
To mingle with those engaged in the precious
Humdrum of shopping.

Man on the Beach

He stands at the edge of existence
Where the nights fall to the gull's call
And the light climbs the cliff of the world
With the birds' song and the time's long
Hope hauled from the depths of the sea.

He walks by himself with no other
Where the winds shake and the waves break
Against the shutters of the silence.
As the tide turns so his heart yearns
To sail where the sea meets the sky.

Yet he knows that he shall never
But must wait for on the longshore
Those who come over the headland
When the world weeps or the light sleeps
To capsize the ship of his longing.

He remembers wandering when a boy
Over sun lit, over star lit
Beaches seeking for a treasure,
A strange sea shell, an old ship's bell
Echoing, ringing tides of tomorrow.

Slowly he turns his back on the sea
Hearing no more the mocking sea-shore
But the earnest, loud voice of his son
From the sea wall, with a new call,
'Daddy, come and sail my boat on the pond.'

Poem for my Four-year-old Son

In these long time days of your growing,
Under the sun spun web of sky,
You stretch with the sea in its yawning
On the long and lazy shore.
Watching grazing gulls in their pasture
Of the rising wave and the fall
You wonder them up with your laughter
Till their milk white flight is your Joy.

Out walking you shepherd your shadow
Through the valleys of the streets
And feed your multitude of sparrows
With your fresh bread heart as it beats.
And harnessed in the eyes of horses
By the sadness of their load
You pull the darkness through its courses
Until your tears release their hold.

When from the forest of your elders
You escape to where the light
Carries you gaily on its shoulders
To the gardens of your sight
You are the child in all the seeing
Of children whose eyes are wide.
Never narrow your eyes of being
And never in our darkness hide.

Regret
for Mark

Now, for the first time, I wish
I had been less dreamer and had worked
Ambitiously for all I could have grasped
Of riches and position to outlast
Whatever demands your pleasure makes.
What more could any father give
Than the greatest subsidy for leisure?
And I can give you none.
I know you love me.
Your love is not in doubt.
But I would feel much worthier if I
Had striven to give you something other
Than a paper strongbox that contains
The small nest-egg of stars I've savaged
From the dark, howling eternity of my heart.

To Chiara

Four and a half is just the age to see,
And only standing two foot three.
The world that's full of hours to wonder
Why this is that, why up and under
So puzzle the dreaming head
And make you stay awake in bed.
It's so worrying and curious
Why grown-up people cry and curse
But smile at you as though you heard
The sweet singing of a little bird.
I see in your dark questioning eyes
A gift only given to the wise.
So just keep on wondering and
The word will be written in your hand.

The Door

To Lindsay in memoriam

Because you do not come,
Because you cannot come again
Into this room of our waiting,
Living through the long day of our hoping
We shall never see
You come again
Into this room
Though our eyes are open.
I know you wanted to come,
Wanted to return.
Four days and nights I watched you
Struggling with the door, struggling
And I could not help you
And only the door between us.
I should have broken down the door
Though it was locked fast against me.
Should have broken down the door
But my hands are only clay
And I knew no way,
Knew no way,
Except my own heart beating
And your heart
Beating faintly through the door
And hoping, hoping -
When it stopped,
When your heart stopped its beating
The door that held so fast
Against the uselessness of hoping,
The door that none could open
Opened to my hand
And I looked through and saw
The empty darkness there and you
Gone through.
Now the door swings shut and open,

Banging in the wind of sleeping,
Letting in the darkness
To this well lit room,
Its lock forever broken.

Still on Their Easy Breath

To my dead daughter

Yes, Lindsay,
I went to see,
They were all there,
Your beautiful and springtime friends,
Boldly breaking another day
From time's interminable delay.
O yes, they were very gay,
Their laughter like a choir,
Their quick and easy smiles like play
And their eyes as clean and open as the sea.
I know now why you loved them,
Why they loved you.
The face of every one was theirs and yours
Perfected by the genius of youth,
Cool and lovely before the sweat of summer,
And its fruit breaks out of innocence.

My shadow fell amongst them,
No, not yours,
I was your dying and your pain,
Your cry in darkness they cannot believe
With their pride of princes in the right to live.

Still on their easy breath the songs
You joined in singing with your laughing mouth
Sound in my ears to the quietness of Aber
And the small pathetic patch I flower
Surrounded by the weeping hills of Wales.

The Doubters

Dad, you know –
What, Son?
Well, Dad, you know some of the kids
Talk about – well, God, Dad
There is no god, son!
I know, Dad, but –
Well supposing there is,
Supposing it's like that book says,
The one they've got in churches,
And he's everywhere.
I've told you, Son, it's not true.
But if it is
I was just thinking,
If it is and I got lost or something
I'd never be alone then, would I?
I mean –
Your Mother and me won't let you
Get lost, Son.
I know, Dad.
But if I did get lost
And there is a God
Well there'd be no need to worry
Because then I never could be really lost
Could I?
Never be alone like –
It would be –
Yes, Son, it would be.

The Guide

No! you do not need me now

To guide you through the easy streets
Of cities where no wild dreams howl
And pride plays with a boy's conceits.

Shake my rough hand from your arm
That steadied you on mountain peaks,
Scorn my tongue that has no charm
Yet counselled you the ways to seek,

Pay me off with gratitude
The current amount in travellers' cheques.
Humble will be my attitude
For nothing more a guide expects.

Nothing more, I watch the sun
Set the mountain peaks on fire,
Their arteries of rivers run
With blood to feed the dreams desire.

Soon I'll watch the dark, cool hand
Of night throw down its dice of stars
And I'll set out for the unknown land
The prophecy of chance inspires.

Poem by Request

For Jeanette, a young French girl

Sexy little urchin your cheeky beauty dares
With the lovely catcalls of your eyes
And the spring-flower swearing of your smile
This late summer Englishman to look
And chase back to his own damp Spring to find
The blazing flower still tender in the uncut grass
And call out hard and fierce love names like regret.

For Bob Miles's Eightieth Birthday

In this eightieth year of your sentience
Still listen to the wind blowing miracles of weather,
The sea surging its song in the ear of the seashell
And all mankind shouting and screaming
Its curses on a forgotten longing.
Watch wisely the demonstrations of clouds
Gathering to their torment of tears,
And the winging birds to their singing nests.
And over in clover, happy in your winter years,
Bless each day as it comes without fear.

Poem for Judith

I would not be so presumptuous to say
I know how you feel or anything that may
Pretend to put myself in your place,
For I can only see me mirrored in your face.
I saw a boy racing driver turn his car
Over this afternoon and tear his face too far
For recognition beyond the bloody red of blood
That made my stomach sick as eating mud.
The common sympathy, like a shower of rain,
Soon cleared as the race continued screaming once again.
To you, that boy what can I say or give?
The worn cliché that babbles on – but men must live?
Of course it's true, clichés so often are,
I mean it's the only truth we know so far –
Courage and the foolish will that has such pride.
God must suspect we have some other sins to hide.

No Way

For Archie MacSporran, on hearing of his death in Africa

There is no way, no way
After the day dawns red
In the sky and a man's born
From the womb of his bed
To choke the curse back
That leapt in the throat
Against the reasoned mind –
Rabbit transfixed by stoat.

Beginning becomes to end
Though we send sad messengers
In mitigation or
Like tourist passengers
Have done to what is done.
The road upon which we're set
Masters reluctant steps –
Smell the fear in our sweat.

I know you always said
Balls to my mysticism
Yet argued in fury
Across your mind's schism.
I know the fears you had
I saw you sweat and ache
And help that I could give
Was only for my sake.

But I loved you, friend,
Though my soft words were harsh
As your harsh ones were kind.
The pity that you asked
You wept out of your heart
In poems that you spoke

And I listened and heard;
Noting that your heart broke

I remember how it was
On hearing my poem read
For my own daughter's death.
It makes me weep, you said.
But nothing that I wrote
Or said or did could turn
Even one event around.
Still hell is where we burn.

Death of a Kitten

Birth had been a struggle.
I watched it break.
Bursting the bubble of unconsciousness.
To breathe the terrible urge to live.
It moved, bewildered by independence.
Crawled, blind, through its mother's fur and sucked.
Life was assured: it was the first victory.
"We cannot keep it. You must drown it, quick."
Two days I watched it live, then found courage.
Death was a struggle.
I watched the close.
A death in water and a stocking shroud.
Oblivion. From which two days before
Life had been released in pain and fearing
Was now a greater fear, a greater pain;
The gift had been accepted and unwrapped.
Now thrown away.

One Hour a Day...

Just one hour a day
Just one hour away
From the loving trouble
Of kids and home and the double
Destiny of father and of spouse
Perhaps I am a mouse
Hiding in my hole in time
A pause between a harsh rhyme
Relief between verse and verse
Of trying and dying to curse
The pink cheeked prince
Who could never convince
My stomach to take
Perhaps I will awake
From the ideal hour
In the tumble down tower
Of a ruined life

But out of the strife
Of order and law and right
I emerge into the light
Of anarchy that takes
Together all possible breaks
To a harmony that's whole
And just for the hour I stole
From the clocked on world
I am free...

Part V: Postcards from here

Written in the Ruins of Ashby Castle

And this dreamer,
Once troubadour who sang his tales before
Patron lords at meat and resting
Between their whoring and falconry for death,
Walks the gloried ruins of their dying
Still making tales to tell another age
That hold his patrons in a pub to listen
And suspend a while their worried worldliness.

By Oil Light and by Candle

By oil light and by candle,
In a pub during a power cut
The shadows, bold out of darkness,
Have presence, like subnormals,
Awkward and ambivalent,
Watching and waiting, frighteningly strange.
And sounds in the soft light allow
Silence to be heard by the young,
Huddling in corners in sexes,
More tender than in the brash light
And noises of their electric culture.
There are no longer marked distinctions
Between generation and generation.
Like an embracing they're together,
Human with human and gathered
In each candle's circle like a charm
To comfort and protect them
Against the encroaching dark.

Where are You Going?

'Where are you going ?' I said to him.
'I'm going' he said, 'I don't know where'.
'Why are you going?' I asked him then.
'Why I am going I do not know.'
He answered me gaily but did not smile.
Then slyly, it seemed, he said to me,
'Is there a reason to go somewhere?'
'That is if there's a place to go!'
I knew not how to make reply.
He smiled at me warmly and passed along,
And I went on my way to where.

Aged Hunter

He knew the coverts and the burrows
Of the rabbits and the foxes
And made his kill in every season,
Poached the private woods of sorrows,
Cared not where the trails he followed
Led, if he could make his killing.

Still he trails where he remembers,
In his pride, the thrill of hunting,
Stalks his quarry till the moment
Of a passion for a killing:
Rises up to strike but listens
To the laughter in the bushes
And knows the death beyond the killing.

Thoughts in a Market Town

I like the faded gentility
Of old hotels in market towns.
I imagine how they strutted there,
The privileged in their ruffs and gowns
And servants fuming in humility
Before each lord and upstart peer.

I like the historic places
Haunted by cold haughty faces
And hot murder in downcast eyes
In lamp and candle shadowed rooms.
I like old churches with their tombs
Of knights and all those plaques of lies.

I like those things because they're past
And applaud their grandiose decline.
The foul sty smell of rottenness
Exudes from all those structures fine.
Yet long shadows that they cast
Touch us still in modern dress.

The Taken

Virgin in her lonely lodging
Lies sprawling on her aching bed
Knees drawn up as in surrender
To princes in her dreaming head.
Shadows and the naked mirror
Are lovers for the eyes to kiss
When lips have never tasted honey
Nor flesh the bee sting of caress.

Through the library of her longing
She seeks the secret of herself,
Fearing the raping ghost of Adam
Rattling the locked door of her youth.
Listening to the wolf wind howling,
Hard fingers of the probing rain,
She snuggles in the bosom pillow,
Child shrinking from her wishing pain.

But the neuter breast of mothering
Cannot comfort her hunger now
She's a woman in her knowledge
Of dreams so sweet they must befoul
The lovely hurt of pure unknowing.
And flushed with the hotter love she fears
She watches in the naked mirror
The last falling of her maiden tears.

High-rise Sonnet

A ghetto blaster mocks the human heart
As monotonous as a workless day.
A woman screams and makes the yelling start
Where home is up a urine-smelling way;
A flat up on the twenty-second floor
With no views of ' those blue remembered hills'
But stark memories of a smashed front door
And cries of fear the aching heart distils
Beat by beat into hatred's prejudice.
A crying baby sucks a soured breast
Nourishing a resigned resentfulness
While Telly's adverts slyly show what's best.
Manic music breaks like bravado sweat
As evening shadows cast their threat.

In the Playground

The playground bully struts around
Frightening all the smaller boys;
'Kicking ass' to show his power,
Boasting to his playgang mates.
Extorting others' pocket money
To buy sweets for his greedy belly.
But a sly one tripped the bully up
And bloodied his nose and hurt his pride,
Then disappeared in the toilet shadows
Where small boys who had suffered most
Sniggered loudly in their delight.
Still the bully rules, he's big and strong
And has so many underlings
To help keep the bully's playground threat;
And there's no teacher to see fair play.

Between Losing and Finding

A boy poised between losing and finding
Pushes his winter way to school
Kicking the stones of his thoughts before him,
His hands sleeping in his pockets like kittens,
Premonitions hunched in his shoulders
And the sun's ghost haunting at his heels.

'This time they will send me away!'
He knew all along and was waiting
Falling into his offence like a hole
Dug especially for him, as before
His brothers fell half relieved and wanting.
Self-sacrifice is a way to revenge
Being born and each day with its burden.
Misery is mitigated by movement
Even if the change is for the worse.
And reason to hate is welcome
When love, soured at the nipple,
Grows to a hard lump in the soft belly.
Tomorrow, does it matter today?
Nothing ends or begins
For the boy between losing and finding.

Laughter

The joy and the boy of the bouncing
Belly of ballyhoo, bursting of seams
And dreams blown on exploding breath
Into a mixture of rollicking
Rainbows and stars and fairs
Of music, with no cares
And no heads to ache.
O the heart's hallelujahs make
Men free and alive and long after
Chuckle the echoes of their laughter ...

You’d Think Spring would make a Difference

A scatter of boys
Enrage a dumb puddle with bricks,
Daring to brave the lash
Of it’s cold, muddied spit in their faces;
And the ugly Siamese twins of houses
Smirk at the sudden photographer of the sun.
Two women in aprons,
Flapping their slippers like seals,
Traipse to the shop on the corner,
With Friday night’s pay in their purses,
Contentedly chewing the cud of their cares.
An old man pushes his grandchild,
Proudly bubbling the noises of infants.
And miners in their garden stalls,
Green fingered with compulsive love,
Bend beneath a roof that can threaten
Nothing worse than a shower of rain.
A dog reads with his nose the small news
And writes with this cocked leg a message.
A girl with her just out of bed face
Swallows the day’s dose of aspirin
To relieve the toothache of dreams.
A man cries out against the world
By shouting fury at a wilful son.
You’d think Spring would make a difference
Coming like a young hero amongst them,
Flushed from his great victory over Winter
And heralding a land fit for heroes to live in.
But they hardly seem to notice the liberation
Though the trees put out flags all around them.
Perhaps they are just afraid of promises,
For they’ve been offered so much by pretenders,
And they can only be certain of paying
More than its value for any gift
And so pretend to themselves there is no victory,
No hero and never liberation

To a land fit for heroes to live in.
So they carry on, as always,
Hiding their feelings behind cynicisms
Like that of their lovers, who
Gear their loves' official consummations
To the tax man's seasonal retrospections.

I've Never Read a Book in My Life

I've never read a book in my life, he said,
Proudly;
Peacock of a narrow world.
Hadn't held in his hands
Knowledge,
Wonder.
Never, turning a page,
Had found
Answers
To unquestioned questions.
He'd never entered a little
The minds,
Feelings
Of men greater than his own.
Turning
Away
From adventures of the soul
He's less
By far
Than everyman's potential.

I Rose Late This Morning

I rose late this morning,
An unusual thing for me,
Did what I had to do,
Without complaining,
And went out, neither knowing why nor where.
Life seemed almost understandable and whole.
The streets and houses, cars and all
The sudden people, caught as though
At a moment of reality, made sense
As in a vision of possibility.
There was nothing alien or strange.
The light and shadows, naked and named,
Were unashamed as lovers after lust,
All sounds, convinced as voices in a play,
Spoke their lines towards the meaning.
I felt as though I could have watched all day
And listened to that dialogue untimed.

Then suddenly I saw
My reflection in a curved shop window.
The frowning eyes the tensed intent of jaw
And my dark crouching predator.
I turned away but all had changed.
The buildings turned their backs upon the street,
The cars unsolved their chaos of pursuit,
The shadows lurked in ambush for the light,
The demagogues of noises ranted hate
And the prey of persons disappeared and hid
Behind the grey camouflage of flesh.
I know, tonight, I'll dream of walking through
The silent desert of my dead
And awaken early to
That false oasis of poisoned light.

The Last Romantic

He, waiting for the rose to come
Out of Spring's green and fragrant mouth,
Discovered Autumn and found it dumb
To call the rose.
He held the pose
Of wonder and waited still to see
The sultry sun deliver
The blood red rose of love to be.

He waited where the sharpest thorn
Bled his fool's heart cynically;
Believing pure out of pain is born
A lovely thing.
But pain can't sing
Except the butchery song of screams
Heard beyond his garden fence
In that wild undergrowth of dreams.

Cooled rivers of late Autumn run
Through the burning, fevered land.
The last season of the rose is done
And grass is tall
And apples fall.
In the roseless garden Winter stands
Cold eyes staring like despair
At the rose bush withered in its hands.

Redundant Man

I grow old without grace,
I the redundant man,
Tending the plants in the public garden
Through the winter of worms
Gnawing at a dead face.

I build day to day stones
A monolith of time,
The bleak totem of my backaching tribe
And stand in its shadow
Amidst obsolete thrones.

I walk through the valley
Of desperate patience
Holding the dangerous criminals in
My love like a prison
Till the mass aunt sally.

I hear the smart vendors
Of wisdom breaking my heart
Into hostile, alien pieces
And dumbly cry the hurt
With obscene words and laughter.

Though I rage in my sleep
Against the naked dream,
The heresy in the private garden
Where the flower comes to bloom,
I rage as if I weep.

I see the brand new ones,
Flash in their cars with girls,
Speaking their slick, factual language of things,
Gaily glib as they pass,
And recognise no sons.

Why? What happened to me?
Did the world get away,
Move to another dimension unseen,
Leaving me with the old
Senses permanently

Of love, hate, joy, sorrow?
A company of ghosts
For the old Adam, cursing in the blood,
To blunder his way with
Blindly to tomorrow.

But there's no road that goes!
All roads come to an end
For the flat earth man who journeys still
In the slow vehicle
Of living as he grows.

Yet my heart beat hope today.
I saw an old man leap
Triumphantly from a fifth floor window.
I knew him before the fall
As the man nought could dismay.

Poem to be Read in a Pub

1

Hey, you there!,
Sitting with your husband, wife, friend or lover,
How did the day go?
Was it a bouncy, bubbling, wide open day,
Stride along humming, whistling day?
Did you make friends, discomfort your foes
With swear words dipped in affection?
Did you find treasure, even discover
Virtue in someone you hated the guts of?
And when you got home was there for supper
A favourite dish you never expected?
You've had a good day.
How about you?
You there, darkening the shadow,
Drinking your hemlock to murder a memory,
Was it really as bad as you're thinking, Or worse?
If so, God help you in drinking!

2

After the morning death in the cold light,
With the warm dreams ghosting and fading out,
The metamorphosis into the flesh,
Bones, blood and the five penal senses
You knock on nerves to test the evocation
And the unmagical materialises into meaning,
Measured in density by your crime to pay.
So you begin your sentence.
An easy term today;
A little anxiety, nothing more:
A child screaming beyond reason for
The loss he thinks a favourite toy,
A twinge of pain to prove you're here,
Though it's hardly needed, but just a hint
To keep you conscious of the politics of punishment

Lest the holiday of sleep made you forget.
A sudden thought from yesterday
Breaks through and wrecks your daydreams of escape.
You smell the wind like mockery,
Turn away and become your daily self.
In sudden panic you look down – but no,
You've not rebelled – you've got your trousers on.
And so you, computer, now switched on,
Operating with a detached and busy hum
Respond to all the stale and stupid stimuli,
Producing the answers you are programmed to.
And yet, despite the day, dreams come dozing in
And for a moment your clumsy hands can hold
A world in a woman's eyes, a child's smile,
And though the pain is there it does not hurt
Or ache, except for its sweet frailty
That your daytime clutching hands must break
At your sudden coming to, afraid
Of love or beauty, happiness or joy,
Knowing the savage penalties they incur.
So you model through, obeying the cogent rules
And listen to that soiled hope, ambition,
Whispering from the echoing cells
Of the committed and condemned.
But the day goes, somehow the day goes
With nothing broken, nothing made.
There's no sudden shot, no blood in the sun,
No scream, no mercy, no evil undone,
No assassin, Saviour, utopian lands,
Just a tired man washing dirt from his hands
Before sitting down to his expected meal.

3

You there, sagely smiling,
Turn your head a little.
What do you see?
A humble of humans, a fardel of fools?

I mean between the covers of our vain who's who.
Or do you see the prideless face of naked man,
Smell his prayer of sweat that once on galley slaves
Or labourers at Pyramids greased the lash of whips?
Or hear his lusts crying through a wilderness of love,
Watch his bruised eyes guard against another blow
And his lips that have worn his words to noises
Fumbling still to find the word, beginning,
That uttered once shall command our patient hands
To shape the key to time's impregnable door
Ten millennia of men have battered on
And enter into the dream of paradise?

4

The evening crowds around us comforting as friends.
The curt curfew of the day is lifted.
And we who were defeated know
Today's survival is our kind of victory.
Tomorrow?
Today's prophecies are the pride of hopelessness,
Blueprints drawn up in the grey workshop of the head.
But we who still have hope's fool courage
Dare to dream only of miracles.

Taking No Notice

He sat there
Taking no notice. No more
Than of the cruising clouds,
The healing laying on of sun,
The breeze taking its roll call of the grass
And the autumn sympathy of trees.
He sat there in the park
Alone on a sadly sunny day
Taking no notice
As he snapped his dry twig dreams
Between hard fingers of his thoughts
And watched some biped creatures
Grazing along the path,
Took no more notice than
They grazed in sets of twos.
He heard a clock count down the hour
Taking no notice except of the after silence
Of waiting to begin again.
He remained there taking no notice till
A dry wrinkled chestnut hand
Fell gently on his own and he
Slowly crushed it, and watched it
Blown by the breeze away.

Nothing to Say

And has he nothing to say, this man,
From his half a century of days,
Nothing more than the tone of his toil
And the sad blue call of his gaze?

For fifty years he's swallowed his phlegm,
That gathering scum of tideless shores.
And the festering cries that would not burst
Corrode his tongue with weeping sores.

O Christ! You thorn fool why don't you scream,
Curse creation, cry anger like flame
Through the cheap 'bargain basement' of dreams?
You hate the maker, seller and shame

Of the wages of angels you've pimped.
The tree you felled in its planted seed
Can give no shade and the sun burns hot
On the hellish wound that refuses to bleed.

Your eyes can't see and your heart can't beat
While you just stare at the empty air.
You know the horror, why don't you shout,
Her soft, white limbs are covered with hair.

And, God the father, that's blasphemy!
But he'll not cry to the end of his days;
Nothing more than the tone of his toil
And the sad blue call of his gaze.

A Man for No Reason

I.
'On the threshold of war!
And so!'
He turns the newspaper over
Reads test match scores and tennis finals.
'England might do well'.
He lets the paper fall,
Looks through the window
And sees the jigsaw sky
And trees and birds unfall
In place to a cheap reproduction,
Draws on his cigarette and blows the smoke
Onto the stage of a sunbeam.
'I'll go down to the coast tomorrow,
Swim in the sea, lie on the beach;
Yea, under the open steps
Pretending I'm asleep and pebble eyed
Look up to the girls descending.
But it'll rain by the look of the sky,
The sea'll be cold and the girls
Wear thick winter knickers.
No! I'll go up to London.
An early train, lunch in a pub,
Heckle the speakers, gawp at the guards,
If it's not raining.
If it is,
Have a nap in the National Gallery.
Then subliminally conned by art
Take in a strip tease, pick up a tart
And catch the last train back, dreading work in the morning.'

II.
'If I get up now I'll be in time,
Be in time. I'll get up when?
Get up when? Get up Gwen!
That's better than working

Even if she's grey as this old morning
And has a voice like whining.
I'll get up now. Get up, For what?
I wonder why, I wonder why
We stand this life and just don't die?'

'I mean. Well what's the point?
Have you ever stopped to think?
Have I ever stopped to think?
Stopped to think of all the people here
And there everywhere like me
Hoping and trying, struggling and cursing,
Praying and neighing dumb as donkeys
For what?
I like to go with a girl, get drunk,
Lie in the sun, dream I'm a millionaire
But then, the dream drops dead,
The sun goes down. There's no escape.
You're stuck with yourself and why and why?
You can't keep living you've got to die
To being the corpse in the coffin of I.'

III.
'I'm getting nicely through life.
Happy, I suppose, one would say.
Yes, I manage quite well.
Nothing elaborate of course.
Moderation is a good maxim
I always say. Everything within reason
And, of course, in the natural law of its season.
Quite right. I am not a romantic
And yet not entirely unromantic.
A good balance I would think,
Life is something of a tightrope,
Don't you think? Love? Hate?'

'Well, I don't know. Overstressed words.
I do get rather fond of people,

And have a strong dislike for others.
But no, I hardly think I would fight,
One way or the other. Well I mean
What would it prove if I did?'

'War? Well against of course!
No intelligent person could be pro-war.
Well it stands to reason.
Hardly worth saying. Such waste.
So disrupting too. I mean
A man wants to get on with his life.
O yes, peace every time.
In such circumstances? That's rather extreme!
I don't really know.
I haven't really thought about it.
Hardly the kind of thing
One wishes to contemplate.
Perhaps, perhaps!
Now, if you'll excuse me,
I must get on.'

IV.
'I'll try, I'll try.
I really will try.
I'll keep a diary
And write down all I do
And say and think and feel.
Keep a record of my life until
I have no need to feel
Or think or say or do
The evil, wicked, dirty,
Stinking, filthy things I do
And say and think and feel.
Keep a record to reveal
The animal in me whom
I shall, by trying hard,
Become.'

The Builder

He chose the site well,
Having in mind the view
Across the valley
Where on clear days the new
Plant, at such distance
Became the fairy castle
He'd dreamed of as a boy
When no birthday parcel
Arrived on hungry mornings,
Or lying cold in bed
He'd stared at darkness
Where loneliness is fed.

He built the house to last,
Stone from the enduring hill,
Timber of resolute oak
And in shape like his will.
Strong, with unbroken front
And a great height for pride.
Within, corridors, a maze
Where a small boy could hide.
And where he had not thought
Shadowed corners in the great
Rooms with brooding space
Like long-invested hate.

When the house was finished
And he came to take his place
As master there, he grew
Afraid and could not face
The going through the gates
Alone. So he looked for one
Who would accompany him
But of those he saw none,
Who would or could enter there.
The sun, smiling that day,
Watched him go through the gates
To the house – the back way.

Cold Corner

He waits,
There on the cold corner,
Hearing the chapel wind
Choir around the gravestone buildings,
Seeing the dark, dumb congregation
Crowd closer to each street lamp altar
And hears a distant clock strike time
As final as a priest's cold voice
Reading the burial service.
And from the sermon of the silence
He takes his text; renunciation
Of her beauty and temptation.

Engaged Couple

Their hands familiar with the holds
Of every tender throw
Submit expertly to each other
Yet never quite win by a fall.
Their eyes, like uncut flowers, glow
Out of Spring's eternal soil
Watered by Winter snows
That in our bitter eyes they know.
Do you love me? Do not hurt me!
Nag our shadows round their smiles,
And standing naked in their sunshine
Our sentimental obscenities.
The mean distance of their short journey
Adds up and down to weary miles
As they walk the petalled road to heaven
In shoes unemptied of our stones.

Doorman's Resignation

Forgive me, sir, I never meant
To be so disobedient;
It is only that I can no more
Stand there watching the swinging door
As one by one each soul goes through.
You see, sir, nothing can I do
For anyone but point the way.
And their eyes, sir, day on day,
Have haunted me. I cannot cry
The stars down from the howling sky.

And they ask such questions, sir,
Humility? The human cur
In genuflection drags the floor.
I'd touch my cap to the painted whore!
Some are naive enough to tell
Me of their lives, they call them hell.
I cannot bring myself to say,
Courage, my friend, you're on the way.
So I can only smile and sweep
Clean the hall where so many weep.

So you see, sir, I must resign.
I've pity and scorn like any nine
Out of ten who enter here.
I know when I leave I shall fear
With them the bleak uncertainty
And yet have hope reborn in me.
And to know no more than they
Is comfort in a foolish way.
Accept, please sir, my resignation
As doorman of your evocation.

The Bugler

By day and dream he waited
While beasts like humans mated
As the heart is full,
Waited through the burning
Summer of their yearning
Till the autumn ghoul
Stole treasures from the dying
And while the breeze, like sorrow crying,
Whispered of their fall.

And flown the summer singers
Left silence to the ringers
Of solemn bells
And the thunderous orators
Of wind's and storm's inquisitors
Who shouted of the hells
To come; while frozen over
Rivers dreamed no pensive lover
With eyes like wishing wells,
And winter's whited fingers
Bit black the hope that lingers
Until the pure snow
Softened the braggart mouth of death.

Again he withheld the breath
Of God to blow upon his bugle
To end their birth and struggle
And their pain to know.

We Look through Glass

The constant motion of water
Under moon and lights of piers
Are visual echoes
Between contrasting darknesses
Of harbour sea.

We look through glass
And meditate on oceans under stars
And refuse all notions of storms and squalls
That could drag us down,
Devouring one by one
Our whole ephemeral human kind.

Land-locked sailors we sit in harbour pubs
And talk swish swashy chat beneath
Nets and oars and unused lobster pots,
Daring no more than rolling to the bar.
By moon-lake waters hearts will only break
To humdrum voices and tinkling glasses,
Where false eyelashes flutter in rank breezes
Of stifling sentimentality.
We'll not brave the ocean to know how
To dare, or kick our pampered mongrel out of doors;
But through double glazing watch the sea,
Unsalted and unwetted, become no more
Than a picture window to sit before
While talking of navigation by the stars.

Ballad of the Boy with a Song

The road that he chose is lonely,
The road that he chose is long,
The girl at his side was bonny
The word on his lips was song.

He possessed no goods or money,
He carried no knife or gun,
The boy with a song like honey
From hives of the morning sun.

A hawk from the sky came diving,
He sang for the mouse a song,
The saddest of songs for living
Creatures that to death belong.

He sang for the death and killing,
He sang for the tears and pain.
His song, for the world too chilling,
Made pity a cry too vain.

He laughed when the girl who loved him
Accused him of loving more
A mouse or a tree or dead thing,
That she he used like a whore.

Then sang he a song of sunshine
That melted the ice away
From rivers and lakes in snowtime
And how a young tree that day

Put out new buds to flatter
The Spring that it felt had come,
But frost in the night was bitter
And struck all the buds' mouths dumb.

She told herself not to listen.
Enraged, she a curse would cry
That night when the moon, arisen,
On his sleeping face was shy.

An oath that is old as loving,
An oath that all women know,
Bring death to his heart and living
If wand'ring his love should go.

The moon and the stars came shining
That night like the dreams that light
A way for the dreamer's mining
Of thoughts that are closed with fright.

And when the white moon his face kissed,
With light that seemed pure and blessed,
She called out in pain and hag hissed
Her curse though her hands carressed.

The boy with a song from sleeping
Awoke the next day to sing
A song of the shadows weeping
For warmth that the sun won't bring.

She knew then that no man or woman
Could hold all his heart or dare
For more than a lovely season
To hope for its fruits to share.

He knowing not friend or other
Was all in the world alone.
For him there could be no lover
But she who the song made known.

Why did You Kill Her, Johnnie Boy?

Why did you kill her, Johnnie Boy?
Why did you kill her as she lay
In your aching, loving arms?
Why did you kill her that bright day
On the hillside of Five Farms?

I know you loved her, Johnnie Boy.
I often heard you speak her name,
Like soft singing of a song,
To bring her to your lovely game
And your eyes swore she'd belong

To you for ever, Johnnie Boy.
Yet when your tender hands caressed
Her face and gently moulded breasts
And fire to fire your lips were pressed
What in your heart changed to beasts

Your hands and murdered, Johnnie Boy?
When she gave so generously
All her lovely riches for
Your joy, what horror did you see
Through the fineries love wore?

Or was it only, Johnnie Boy,
She called you by some other name,
Dreaming in her pleasure pain
Of some past lover who made claim
To her heart, as flowers to rain?

But when we found you, Johnnie Boy,
It seemed you'd put the world to rest.
You smiled with such strange content,
A man who'd passed some gruelling test
To know of manhood's full extent.

You never told us, Johnnie Boy,
Why you killed her. You did assert
'I had to' as though you'd saved
Each man of us from some great hurt.
Like a hero you behaved.

But you'd not tell us, Johnnie Boy,
The secret that you took to death.
We were childen who'd not known
The prisoner shackled in your breath,
Horror guarded all alone.

Yet now they've hung you, Johnnie Boy,
The sun shines out across Five Farms,
Shadows on the soft green hill
Are smiled away, and in their arms
Lovers take each other still.

Passing Images

Dawn breathes slowly over the land
And the world develops
From the negative of night
And emerges to the clear print of day.
A new day, a new birth,
The bud of a plant
Opening in a season
Of indifferent weather.

Clouds like the fists of gods
Threaten the earth
Till the absolution of rain
Clears to forgiveness.

Count not the hours
For life is in each second
Glorious in its coming and passing:
Wind over water on a sunny day.

I watch the water lapping the shore,
Like a spent lover still caressing
The sated land, on a summer's day.

I see a small child slowly smile
Like a new knowledge come to the mind.

A young woman, tight trousers
Flaunting buttocks and hips,
Reveals the true genius of creation.

These are an old man's images,
Come to the mind like pictures
In galleries of forgotten towns,
On an ordinary day, of an ordinary life.

Postcard from Here

No bikini girls display
The male thought of the way
To heaven. Only the sand grinds
In the mill of the waves
To desolation.

The sun breaks through like pain.
But mostly the rain weeps
On the shoulder of the land
And the wind mocks the placid sea
To spitting curses.

The sullen crowds of cliffs are dumb
To answer demagogic winds'
Whispered or screamed incitement,
Though forces of the sea
Furiously attack.

Here there is nothing sugar sweet,
Sea salt has a taste like blood
Upon the bitten lips.
Gaiety would be cheap wine
At an alcoholic's blind.

Genius of gulls' wings write
Their poetry of flight
But their desperate screech of need
Breaks the self forgetfulness
Faculty to heed.

The one long line of footsteps
Leading across the sand,
Showing I was here today,
At the next tide's turning
Will be washed away.

Part VI: Mining Poems

Just Another Dark Day

The alarm batters out the brains of my dreams and the corpse obediently and slightly in panic turns off the clatter and dragging the clock beneath the bed clothes lies tensely counting the tick-tocks that fall, in the half dawn darkness, onto the coffin lid of another day.

I feel a twinge of rebellion, but after so many years of control it is born dead and it's wizened face changes into an expression of self pity and my mind turns over to the side of resentment and stokes up the fires of rage against society, my job and in the worst of all possible worlds, having to rise at four thirty a.m. to begin again the torture of the day's work.

I crawl out of bed, my rage beaten by my cowardice and pull on my clothes. My mind blank, my stomach a bit queasy with dumb apprehension. I descend the stairs, obediently being quiet, for waking the kids or my wife would be an act of selfish assertion against the law of necessity. I enter the cold kitchen and put on the kettle, make the fire, burn the toast by some ant-like reflex and slump in a chair to drink my tea, feeling as weary as a wagon wheel grinding up a rutted farm road and blanking off thoughts of another working day.

I cycle slowly to the pit my resentment shading the early morning light, my ears hearing the chorus of birds like the jeers of the fortunate. In the pit-head baths I change into my work clothes smelling their sharp coal dust, sour sweat smell and know I'm putting on the shirt of Nessus. On the pit bank I smoke a cigarette before going into the cage and down.

Fourteen men sardined into a cage dropping into the dark, each with his secret thoughts. At the pit bottom we stream off the cage faced with the queue of men from the night shift waiting to ascend. One of the men from the cage greets one of the men from the night shift with 'Hello big prick', came the instant nonchalant reply, 'Your wife's been talking again'. The man from the cage does not reply. The going up and going down changes the moods of men like a manic depressive. I get on the small train that takes me and all the other men on the early shift towards their work.

Pit Man

Of course he's quite subhuman,
Pit man, twentieth century.
Works hard, gets dirty,
Uses a shovel and pick,
Often in danger,
Strong, horny-handed,
Foul-mouthed,
Stubborn, aggressive
Only if too far provoked.
No social graces,
Conservative in habits,
Stupidly loyal,
Even to socialism,
Drinks, gambles,
Monogamous, mostly,
Generous, meaning
Hard come, easy go.
Derogatorily humble,
Great sense of humour,
Wisely at himself.

Near a Colliery at Dawn

They have awakened a century of dawns
Those heavy booted feet, clogged or hobnailed,
Of men in dour and dust black uniforms
Marching to the front line of their war.
These unbemedalled soldiers of no renown,
In the great battlefields of Yorkshire and of Wales,
Scotland, Durham, Leicestershire and Notts,
Down to the little skirmishes in Kent.
This army, recruited from the sons of fathers
Breathing bitter dust down the generations of their strength,
Born to the shovel and the sweat,
Darkness and danger lesser men would cry
Their cherished dreams out for self-pity's sake.
And as they march, still spitting the last shift's dust,
Their muscled bodies shouldering their aches.
They shoulder too the dead weight of the broken
Who shift in wheelchairs for their working days
And spend long nights buried beneath their fallen sky.
And perhaps the silent thousands,
Who saw the square sky shuttered down
For the final shift to darkness, now return
To share the old companionship of fear
Clenched tightly in a blue scarred fist or heard
As silence between the laughter and coarse talk.
The headstocks, like gallows, from which a cage is hung
Is still the symbol of a mystery;
Another world, a monastery that holds
Its rites in work made catacombs that daily fall.

Rising for the Early Shift

Four thirty and no sign of morning
Yawning over Ashby hill.
The will is weak. Who's for dreaming
Still sleeping in the warm bed burrow,
Nest of skylark or nightingale who blessed
The trees' strict meditation evening past
And cast a fiddle sadness for a catch
Of stars? O who's for dreaming
Of the golden girl whose eyes have visions
Of your greater worth, of the birth of luck
To load the laden heart with lighter things;
With wings and song and gifts of God to wrong
The ringing, shattering bell you curse in Hell?

Who's for dreaming? But the spell is cast.
The witch of shadows falls
Across the face beside you as you switch
The light for seeing in the dark.
The dream is gone and wistful wishing's torn
By the savage light to show the creditor of time
And all who beat upon your crowded door
In the name of those who claim
Salt from your sweat and tears.

Another stint, another day to go!
You measure out your life in coal,
Adjust your vision to the dark
For crawling where the menacing wall
Shall keep you sweated prisoner.

There you'll pray with song or curse or spit
The dust from out your throat and hope.
For what? Ten thousand pounds or just
The warm sun on your face or night

So you can sleep again and start
As bird or beast or man to rise
From bed or burrow, nest or field
To watch the liberating light uncover
The world the fall of night had buried.

Waiting to Descend

We get our lamps and wait five minutes, ten,
In the unused, lung clean, morning air,
Before we go to the shaft and down.
We drag last cigarettes and sit
On powder tins, clubbing together
Against some threatening hurt and hear
Our piebald language grin and fling
Our life back in our pale and tired faces
That sleep has failed to quite repair,
Resenting softer men still in their beds
Turning over and grunting across their wives
Some hollow sounding blasphemy of ease.
We joke as coarse as emery cloth
To round the sharper edges of our spleen
And cough up phlegm with laughter
Black with dust and curses to spit out.
Then flipping carelessly our fags and dreams
We pick up powder tins and slouch
Across the first reluctant stint of light,
The sky free birds have whistled up,
And enter the cage where whistling's never heard.

Up from the Day Shift

We come blinking out of the dark,
Shy as children, lifting our eyes
In the great ceremony of the sun,
Our hands clutching our lamps
As though we still have need of them;
Perhaps uncertain of being allowed to stay.
We straighten our backs and walk
Upright across the careless yard
Sure with each hurrying step
We got in without being noticed.
And so our day begins,
Wakening wide from a double darkness
With light to squander in half a time.

Pit Fall

A prop broke,
Came the earthquake from above
And the edge of doom
Catching me just askance
Flung me aside
As though not wanting me
This time.
So it is, perhaps, that fate decides
In that stopped second
Whether one should live or die.
Looking at my blue scarred fingers
Across some thirty years
I wonder why the fall
And my escape.

A Prayer for All Miners

Hell and shit,
Bloody Christ, the
Pain and all fucking glory
And cunting of things
Earth open and swallow
The green, golden blasphemous
Vomit of its womb.
And 'I' will be done
In the dust, choking a breath
Once breathed in the sea air breeze.

I will not behold you man
Standing in your trembling rage,
Shaking in my muscles and bones
To the edge of the black silence
Of nothing in the day's
Climax of a castrated pit mood.
I will not hold you to be done,
Admit, confess, recognise one bead
Of blood or sweat
On your ignobly infinite brow.

You will be done ever and ever,
Amen, to the last sinew and gasp
Of the whole gaping wound to the last
Dropping of seed in the hole
And bury and cover with dust
The great black encompass your arms
Ache to reject and hold.

Miner's Death

'Joe's been buried!' The call came
Cracking the whip of the heart,
Crying cold like wind on sweat
And we shivered knowing our part;
Fed pity's hungry mouth with pain
From the blow of a dirty oath
Forgiven in humbling knees that crawled
Our prayer to the merciless earth.

With our hands, loving and hating,
We shifted the senseless stone,
Our eyes cursing the brooding roof
While we cowered in our flesh and bone.
When hope stood back we found him
Beneath a stone eight feet by four
And eighteen inches thick. We told
His Mass in tears of sweat and for
A hymn our silent curses sang
To the organ music of our breath
As we broke the stone and saw
The remains of the feast of death.

The crushed thing in a clothing shroud
We rolled for the funereal journey through
The ways of darkness into the light.
There the sun shone and flowers grew
In the blessed earth as on the day
First the world was offered us.
We blinked the darkness from our eyes
From our hearts the poisoned pus
We drew to leave the deep wound clean;
As in truth's time we gazed again
On the shrouded thing that held
All our darkness and our pain.

Poet Miner

I crawl through all those galleries of contemplation
Where silence speaks like thought to thought and every
Grain of dust is dehydrated being,
Where mood on mood of time and calm and storm
Colour, shape, design's compressed into the mind
That holds the secret of the first beginning.
Slowly I go, for here I know the hand
Clutching to right the stumbling foot may tip
The balance of the world when every prop's
A set pretence to hold up doom.

I stare from my oasis of brackish light
Into the Sahara of dreadful darkness
And know that in that death of seeing eyes
Is sight and in that darkest darkness light.
For as day is born of night so shall my sight
Be born of blindness.
But I remain within my lighted cell
Dragging my lamed existence, Oedipus like,
Along the ways of artificial light
And keep my love imprisoned in my heart,
Blowing dreams like bubbles in the air
To burst against the walls of this my hell.

Unfinished Dream

When working as a miner I had this dream
Of working at the coal face when
My lamp picked out a narrow opening
In the pit wall,
An unsupported fissure, unplanned
And unsure.
I took my courage in my hands
And entered there, unthinking
As unknowing where it led.
Then, as I moved along the darkened way
A dim light came and led me on
Till I came out to sunshine
On a sandy beach with salt sea air.
Though all was amazement, I was not surprised
Because a dream can be a promise long foretold.
At the edge of the shore was a longboat
With four sailors at the oars
And standing at the helm was an officer
Who greeted me with acclamation.
I took the seat he offered me,
Then the boat was rowed away.

Part VII: Freedom

Freedom

Would she be ours if we had loved her more?
Seems strange
The noble ones who loved her most she never loved at all.
I wonder why she runs
With trembling breast from we
Who see her always on some distant hill,
Shy as the wild gazelle and free?
Perhaps she knows our vanity
That bedecks our loves in chains
And claims what we ourselves can never give
And knowing this runs like any hunted thing
From the hunter who
Pursues.

Shouting from a High Place

In any temple of the gods
Or court of confidence
I refuse
To swear my allegiance to
Their laws.
Or, subservient to the wrongs
That they decree,
Condemn my blood,
My tongue
To confessions of false humility.

On this last freedom
I will stand
A man
Without philosophies to bind
My love
Or sanities to sterilise
My fecund foolishness.
Only how I love
In these dimensions shall I be
Until I cry enough
And then
Their death might comfort me.

Before We Go Under

But before we go under let us name
All those who are to blame
Under the earth, the sea and under
The sky. Let us name them in one;
All who have lived and died under the sun
Before us, for us and within us.
Let us name those who shall die by us.

And before we go under let us pray
Not for our sins or the virtues of they
Who led the way into temptation
Through the ornate door, but in meditation
Let us say to the shadow, to the ghost
Forever and before you are our host
Containing us and yet never restraining
Our will during the time in your house.

Before we go under let us forget
Not how young we were born to beget
Man responsible in his acts and aware
Of the day to come after the great despair
But let us forget all that has been done
And undone and this evening without shame
We shall walk with our children calling the lame
From crippled shadows, the dying from death
And the word of praise from our prison breath.

The Afflicted

You've made the world and lost
The promised
Land we've not found:
But you will never know
The hope that we shall find.

You in your perfumed cell
Of cry proof,
Shock proof concern
Never breathe the pure air
We smell as faeces foul.

This is our affliction.
We must breathe to suffocate
In air fouled by sewerage
From scented sanctums of despair.

We faint, fall to sickness.
Recover
With a built in
Immunity that makes
Us fit to go on breathing

Your rank, polluted air
Of freedom.
We cry again
Silence against your world
And catch the bounced back pain.

We the afflicted are
The bastards,
Sons of Ishmael,
The lost unchosen ones
To cry our hurt to be heard.

Tomorrow will be
No silence.
Wounds shall be healed
To the red scar's hate
Dumb with the noise to kill.

And Some Young Man

And some young man,
Smiling on his way to heaven,
Proudly walked his purpose
Into the crowded restaurant
And so committed switched to death.
What grim god commands a boy to make
Such sacrifices on the altar
Of the pride of ages?
The torn bodies of children
And other men can never be
Praise to any sanctity.
And after the deaths
The hatred explodes
Into shrapnels of fear,
Piercing the mind
To black holes of despair
Where only revenge can relieve the pain
For a brief moment
Before the holocaust.

Incident with Child

What are they massing for?
Father, why are they massing,
Massing? Now they're moving this way.
See them, Father, moving
This way and towards our house!

Why are they coming here?
Father, why are they coming,
Coming and all shouting our name?
Hear them, Father, shouting
Our name like a word of hate!

Why are they calling us?
Father, why are they calling,
Calling us and swinging their sticks?
See them, Father, swinging
Their sticks like lion tamers!

Why are they wanting us?
Father, why are they wanting,
Wanting us for hurting so much?
Why us, Father? Hurting
Us will not cure their pain.

No one is stopping them!
Father, no one is stopping,
Stopping them! They're breaking the door.
Stop them, Father, breaking
The door down into our house!

But there is nothing can.
Father, no, there is nothing,
Nothing can. They're breaking the door
Down now, Father, Breaking
The door that guarded our dreams.

My Ghosts

The ghosts that haunt me are the living
Skeletons of famine
The victims of the unforgiving
Of past and present time.
They haunt me all those ghosts of war
The ones who couldn't fight
And fled inescapably before
Such tyranny and might.

In the haunted houses of my mind
Ghosts of the unloved weep
And screams of terror, to shame mankind,
Shatter the calm of sleep
And those grey spectres that point my guilt
I shall not exorcize
Till the vilest blood of men is spilt
In the gutters of our lives.

The Conqueror

After so long, when we had almost thought
Our endeavour lost, our dream defeated
We marched in triumph through their city
Bearing our standard proudly amongst them.
So many lined the streets to cheer us
That we imagined our victory was complete
And never more to be contested.
For this, we thought, is the final victory
That none can doubt or ever twist about.
These thoughts we had and dreamed of a new becoming
That would draw from the old roots' maturity
Strength to resist the elements of evil
And, forming fresh shoots, flower into beauty.
This was the foolish dream we dreamed forgetting
All the things we had done and undone.
But when we returned to trace the way we'd come
We saw across the mighty track of time
A great dividing chasm none could bridge
And on the other side the old world lost.
The wounds of war in many would not heal
And festered to a gangrenous despair.
Many there were who wept for their lost homes.
Even the strong were sad for in their hearts
Home was like memory of innocence
That smiled upon an old embittered face.
And the unimaginative found it touched
The aching day with faint dream fingers.

But we who were too young to die for loss
Or dream, we who longed to live and love
And had the courage to believe that birth
And death are not vain cancellings out to keep
A balanced ratio between mouths and food,
Or the secrets held by all the worlds
Not just a hoax to bedevil man

And mock his reaching hands with emptiness,
Turned our backs upon the gap in time
To begin the journey all must take
Who, having won the battle of their age,
Know that defeat is the only conqueror.

Poem for an Astronaut

And on these pale light evenings into night
Become a lover at your garden gate
And hold the quiet, darkening houses tight
And spell out home, as children on a slate
Mark the new wonders of the alphabet,
With the first stars, for fear you shall forget.

Walk your way through the crowded town below
And recognise yourself before you go
To other worlds to seek what you believe.
For in a thousand faces you will find
An image of the man you can't deceive
Who knows you only leave the stars behind.

Silent before yourself, making the down
Count to the last zero of your truth,
Tremble to the live green and dead brown
Of seasons with their withering and their growth,
Know the fruit you ate from your father's tree
Retch up its seeds and plant reality.

No Change Yet

And always it has been
The land our betters made
Grey, grim and underlean
And never overpaid.

As always now it is
The harassed mother's face
Her love a tight-lipped kiss
And nothing worth the grace;
The rise and fall of days
Through all the century years.
A history to raise
A brood of civic tears.

Nothing has changed so much
To make the heart beat quick;
The cripple needs his crutch
And medicine the sick.

And in our chapel hearts
We wear the Sunday clothes
Designed by actors arts
To hide our flesh that glows.

The painted clouds obscure
The golden place and light,
As pasteurised the pure,
Democracy the right.

But from the garbage bins
We sneak a crust of bread
And sauce it with the sins
Against the holy head.

And so we do not starve,
But many of us are weak
And need a lead to carve
The new shape that we seek.

But who shall give the word?
A Diogenes of art
Abusing the human herd
With love to break the heart?

Workers

What are they digging for
Those workers in the dust,
Striving and slaving there
Between sunrise and dusk?

I watch and wait to see
The object they will gain
But see only the sweat and dirt
Hiding a gleam of pain.

And so the day wears on
Without respite or call
Of triumph, they just heap the dust
Each one and build a wall.

More and more they dig
And the wall grows wide and tall
Till I can see no more
One worker there at all.

What Would I have Done?

I would not willingly have done those things.
Joined to obey, supported that company,
Acquiesced, by thought or deed of smaller evil,
Within the all consuming evil of the total sin.
No, I would have held my breath and burned
My thoughts to ashes to scatter on the graves
Of all the persecuted and worn the weeds
Of mourning for the death of my lived life.
But what would I have done if forced to live,
Participate? What would I have done
If given the violent, savage choice
Only between executed and executioner?
If they had forced me to go where
Their victims waited for my brotherhood
Or my hand to strike them down;
My brotherhood beside them in their dying
Or my manicured hand to sign,
Turn the gas taps or burn their fleshless bones.
What would I have done?
If they'd taken my own son as hostage
To terrify, transport in stinking cattle trucks
Amidst all the jazz of screaming flesh
To the last moment of forgiveness
They forever cursed their sons to lose
If I failed to terrify, transport and murder
Sons of other men who'd put my own son past forgiveness?
What would I have done?
Tear out my heart from feeling,
Put out my eyes from seeing,
Wither my flesh till no pleasure
Or pain can touch one dried nerve's end,
So the relentless interrogator of the blood
Shall no longer question to discover
The answer to my feared cowardice.

The Patrol

Carrying their fragile hope,
Balancing life on death
As a walker on a rope
Controls his trembling breath,
Across where friends were slain
The patrol moved through the rain.

Their hands of courage held,
Just like the frightened nurse
Who keeps the insane quelled
With strong arm blows and curse,
The fear they knew would start
To scream within the heart.

The enemy was still,
It seemed the quiet night
Had forgotten how to kill,
Even the rain was light,
Like fingers of warm tears
Caressing sorrows years.

And all the world asleep
Was dreaming like a child,
Not knowing men must creep
Past dreams into the wild
Stretches of a nightmare
And see death from its lair

Rise up and sniff the blood
Upon the hands of war
And crouching in the mud
Make ready with its claw
To strike the unchosen down
Like a rag and paper clown,

There, through the fantasy
Of shapes and shadows moved
The shrinking memory
Of all that they had loved,
But none can recognise
A truth before it dies,
Balanced through the night
On the line that runs between
The shadow and the light
Each man had known and seen
Where his hell is born,
The patrol returned at dawn.

A Brave Man knows His Coward's Risk

To give in now would be to prove
That all they speak of mediocrity is true.
But worse!
I'd fail my genius and lose
Even the man it led me to.

A brave man knows his coward's risk,
Sweats camels through the impossible needle's eye
But spits
Contemptuously in the face
Of any king thumbing him to die.

A Kind of Explanation

So I must explain from the start,
Tell the full story.
You see I could not bring myself
To believe
The sweet fables of the heart.

The story's ordinary enough.
Told in the dead lines
Of a million faceless faces.
The fables?
Remember the gob stopper stuff?

Perhaps you were less fortunate,
Did not question right
Of princes, witches' destruction,
Lovers who
Never sweated out their hate.

After each fable I still heard
The witches' laughter.
Though I stopped my ears against
Their curses
I caught the one spellbound word.

And so I never belonged
To right mindedness,
Dreams made before the age of five
So three score
Years and ten could go unwronged.

I've paid, believing not quite right,
With witchless laughter
At my incongruous vision,
From princes
With love bitterer than spite.

Still I have what they now think absurd,
The witches magic
Given, though I stopped my ears
To curses,
Given in the spellbound word.

To explain myself as poet,
This necessity
Has long dragged at my mortal heels,
For myself,
Perhaps, to understand it.

So early you marked me stranger,
Stood me in a corner
Wearing your stupidity
On my head.
Your classroom was my manger.

The oxen, asses of my thoughts
Were friends in wonder
Who rode me through the blank, dead wall
Of seeing
To the fields my vision sought.

Out of myself I went, became
Vision unfolding,
As a leaf to the sun, the other self
Of seeking
Called and broken out of shame.

Even in my sleep escaping,
Knowing I escaped.
For I rose out of my sleeping form
And looked down
Upon the worldly aping.

Soul escaping the cell of flesh.
But every man
Of course must wrap a noise around
The silence
And from the darkness net his silver fish.

A Reasonable Plea

O for Christ's sake, Dad, they are your children!
And it's about time you took the worst in hand.
We know, Dad, you don't easily condemn
But you promised we'd inherit our land,
Yet how shall we when they, our brothers,
Have ferreted out your secrets, to destroy?
God, Dad! We, your meek sons, know our brothers.
They'll not stop. Remember? You said, they would employ
The death they commanded in their hands
Upon themselves. Dad, if you don't intervene
It will be them and us and all our lands
One bowl of ashes. Dad, you'll see the scene,
Waking up one eternity, and then
You'll wish you'd been firmer with your sons of man.

The Cry

We move into a new millennium,
Miracle, magic, moonshot for man.
Of course it cannot be believed
For unbelievable is prophecy
When all the prophets are but fools.
And fools know not the thought
Their words unknowing come to say.
Words heard in the sea song
And the song's song, the roar of traffic
And the way men die of youth.

I saw a film against war,
I saw a film against sex;
The old film, the same film
Made since all films were.
A no cry about life and death.
O the cry, the cry
Caught in the throat of time.

I've heard a voice say what it could not say
And say it until I heard
My voice cry what it could not cry,
A word no longer truth
Nor lie.
To believe and disbelieve
I sat on the seashore and listened to the sea,
I walked in the city, a cold March day,
Remembering how it was to grow,
Forty years ago or more,
To hear the sea's song and the fool's song
And know the cry.

Even though they crack the heart
And suck out the tender tenderness
To leave it wizened like a fig,

Dried in some fiercer than tropic sun;
Even though they take the brain
And pick it nervously to bits,
Like the frayed straw bag
Owned proudly by that old hag
In our geriatric mental wards;
Even though they mix the blood
With excremented media,
Show black is white and in between,
Twisting the spectrum's arm to scream,
The pain and terror as we die
Will gasp out a kind of song to cry.

The seagulls fly above Spithead
Wheeling, wheeling in the sky,
Crying, crying as though they die.

I heard an old man on his boat
By the Camber singing out
His song of praise.
Seventy-nine years old and young
He sang, working in early March about
His shipshape sailing boat.
Last year, they said, from the quay
Onto his boat eight feet he'd leap.
He knows a grave is six feet deep.
In the sailors' bar on Camber quay
The talk's of nothing but the sailing way.
The low life bastards come and go
Cursing, drinking in a row,
Almost as though they live to die.
You see it in their salient eye,
Praise as sun on wind taut jib,
Hallelujah! As though the ebb
Tides turning and their ship is stored
Ready for sailing when they go aboard.

II

March blows warmer
And Winter with a sheepish grin
Shrugs off its defeat by Spring.
Fool of all fools starts to sing
Dancing to the eternal tune,
Believing the blossom and the birth,
Smiling at the girls and boys,
Forgetting life destroys, destroys.
Eternity and all that lore
Is a horror fairy story for
Mankind's children suffering through
Their stint of three score years and ten.

III

Put up the prisoner, called the clerk.
A thin, bald man of middle age
Was ushered in.
The Assize judge in his crimson gown
And wig of sophisticated sin
Gazed at the prisoner and noted him.
From all his papers the clerk read out,
Name, address and crime alleged.
The judge, the barristers, all concerned
Listened and like the prisoner heard.
Each man shuffled in his skin,
The prosecuting counsel rose,
The case before the court began.
The prisoner like everyman
Sat down and listened to
The evidence and in between
The silence and absurdity,
Between the accusing words,
The circumstantial evidence, the facts,
The pleas, all throughout the trial,
Despite the sentence, despite the crime,
Between, a kind of mockery, a glee,

A predisposition untutored yet,
Towards a knowledge and certainty
To make the judge and prisoner, all
One guilty innocent who had to fall.
And each man afterwards alone
In his cell of skin and bone
Hears the cry and says, perhaps,
To friend or stranger 'hear that bird?'
Doesn't it sing, so beautiful!

Sitting here alone at peace,
Unheeding the world around but knowing it,
The cry becomes, the sound's embodied,
The inarticulate's expressed.
I am caught and held, momentarily,
Against my cowardly will
And feel the vision of reality
Tearing my human credulity,
Lifting me, calling me out,
Charging me to dare, just answer
That I am aware.
But the tension crumbles, the vision fades,
The call becomes no more
Than disbelief, that comfortable relief.
The world crowds round me
Like welcome old false friends
Understood and forgiven because they're known.

This Street

Outside this street I knew I'd be
As free within my world as free
Birds that in secret sanctuaries
Wing wild or stilled in deep nests lie
Contemplating from towered trees
New flights into the boundless sky.

Beyond this street was every dream
That as a youth I could esteem
And mine if I had passed and ceased
To know what here holds every sound
Of bitter weeping unreleased
For joy discovered but not found.

So I remained and listening heard
Deep in the silence of that word
Another dream that sang of love.
And in this street I learned to be
A willing prisoner knowing that
The loveless and the lost are free.

The Day After

No, Son, the day after we said,
But, Father, tomorrow will be
A fine day. Look the sky has bled!
Remember, Son, we did agree
Upon the day after, and tomorrow
Though its promise is fine cannot borrow
More than hope from the day after.
I know, Father, only today
Has been so long without laughter.
And now is there a need to stay?

Tomorrow, my Son, we shall know.
What can happen, Father, between
Today and tomorrow or grow
Enough to alter this one scene
To happiness. You know, Father, as I
There's nothing to stay for except to die.
There is a way to live, my Son.
And here, today and tomorrow,
Should we not make our will be done,
Distilling laughter out of sorrow?

And the day after, my Son,
Cannot come till tomorrow is done!

Explanation

Let it not be said
I have forgotten
The red lips that bled
To a pale thin line
Of love dead.

Let it not be thought,
Despite self pity,
I've taught myself short
Of blaming my hand
Where it wrought

The cast iron sneer,
The cold, love twisted
In-tear to appear
Beyond or above
My despair.

The hurt I have done
Laughs in the deep wound
The one heroes shun
And cowards inflict
As they run.

I say the regret
Slowly out of heart
And let meaning set
Problems I must face
To forget.

Do not ask me why.
No answer is true.
I sing, as I lie,
Requiems to a truth
That can't die.

Part VIII: The Human Condition

Narcissus Reflects

Once Narcissus gazed and thought
'How clear and beautiful my face!'
But after many hours he sought
A stone to throw into the place.

The mirror of the waters broke,
Then from the depths the sludge did rise
And all the horrors that awoke
Were mirrored in his frightened eyes.

A Song for No Reason

Here's a song for no reason.
Not for love nor its season
Is this song that I sing.
It is, perhaps, as bells ring,

Sun shines, water flows and time
Flies, as my being in rhyme.
My toil puts bread in my mouth,
For life that's never enough.

No reason to sing have I
Though many reasons to cry.
Yet out of my heart comes a song
For no reason of right or wrong.

Impressions, Late Evening

A door bangs in the sudden wind,
The trees in the garden shiver
And the colour of flowers dissolves
In the solution of late evening,
Only their scents fingering the senses.
I breathe cooled air and watch lights
From dusk-shrunk, timid houses,
Stare no dreams out of darkness.
A dog barks. The woman next door
Noisily bolts her house against
The knowledge of the lonely.
A sports car changes gear for the corner,
Its voice breaking to solicit
Dreams of youth to follow.
A child's cry aches to a man's laughter
And my imagination dribbles,
Like an idiot boy,
Drooling over a wonder the sane find inconsequential.
The cool air touches my skin through my summer shirt
And I go slowly into the house
As though returning after a long absence
With an alien bride brought from a far land.

Every Man Knows

Every man knows
What's under a woman's skirt
But looks every time she lifts it.
So it goes,
The rose perennial in the light
Of bushes and overflows
The river in its pride
Of water, knowing it can flow.
All that I shall know
I have known with everyman
Who knows the eternity
Of knowledge before it grows
To know.
I say it and say it again,
The pain and the pleasure are
Seeded by the same stone
Of the miracle of wonder.

Expedient Man

I will not, shall not finally accept,
Turn my back for ever on, defect or –
No, that would be tantamount to suicide.
I shall pretend, act the part, bend,
Graciously of course, use tact,
Speak their language conform to rules,
Keep my face exactly straight to please
Their seriousness and laugh, of course,
In the fashionable places, shout the names,
Make the signs and only when I'm absolutely sure
There is no danger,
Act as they think is right.

At the Roundabout

Being confronted with so many roads
We stopped, puzzled and confused,
Realising we did not know which way to go
And had no knowledge of the roads ahead.
All the roads were different from each other
Only, it seemed, in the direction which they led,
For there was no indication of their destinations
Where they radiated from one centre.
We studied the roads for a long time
Trying to understand the meaning of their ways.
Circle on circle we made
But were unable to choose or know
Which road was the road we should take
Until even the road we came
We confused with the others
And if we'd tried taken the wrong road back.
So we wait, camped on the great roundabout,
And gaze along the roads with no signs,
Telling our tales of hope we hardly believe in,
Comforting ourselves with our little loves,
Passing our time with games of endeavour
Within the worn-out arena we dare not leave.
Some travel round and around the circle
No longer seeing the roads that lead
In so many directions to give
Impossible ways to arrive
At the destination we started out for,
Telling themselves, here is the end and beginning
And there is nothing for us beyond
This eternal, repetitive circle.
So we wait and shall wait until
A sport, with no courage to care,
Starts us again without reason
Casually on any of the roads from here.
Then we shall be on the next leg of our journey.

Many, of course, will remain,
Caring too much for their kind,
Seeing in the reflection of others
The glory of their own image to worship,
Incestuously perfecting themselves
To the specification of destruction.
But we, who'll drift after the sport
On the current of our colloquial blood,
Cursing the road and the way,
Knowing no peace or content
Shall journey forever along,
On roads we have no reason to go,
The way that has no sign to convey
A destination.

The Fall

After the long day, long before
The sore thumb counting of time,
When we walked together and were
One with the trees of praise
That raise exultant arms to heaven,
And running rivers
Racing over rapids fell to our thrill
And crashed – converted into calm
Swan sliding ease
That was our peace with the
Sheep moving fields
Slowly and holy
As a congregation of corn,
We saw the sudden horses thunder from shadows
And we dreamed – alone.

Poem

The beauty of the flower invites
The bee's rape; to procreate.
Is beauty a lovely truth
Or lie made up by human eyes
To colour lust?
Is the ravaging and savaging
Of Nature just a balancing
Between the seed and the gut?
Is love our precious flower
Devoured by a carnal appetite?
But if after lust love comes,
Sweet and gentle as wild flowers
Or like the lowering of the sun
To an evening, serene as trees
Painted by the light of sunsets;
We forget.
When love comes, its beauty is believing
As eyes of children trusting
Who have not yet been betrayed;
We forgive;
Or spin into spirals of doubt.
We can only live with a moment
Poised between yesterday and tomorrow.
And its truth and beauty a passing
Like a butterfly on the wing.

The Wall

Every day he goes into the garden
And looks at the wall he has built,
So straight and true, the day before.
Then, after a while, in contemplation,
He breaks it, brick by brick, to its foundation.
Then he begins again, with the same bricks,
To build once more, as straight and true,
An identical wall on the same foundation,
No one knows why he builds the wall
Each and every day alike, to fall,
It seems to have no purpose one can see,
Either as shelter, guard or privacy;
Just six feet long and four feet high,
A double bricked, strong yet useless wall.
If you ask him why he builds the wall
He will not answer but plumbs it true,
His craftsman's hands mocking you.
Or if you say – 'Why knock it down?'
His eyes will neither smile nor frown
As he replies, 'So I can build it up again,'
So he builds up the wall to fall,
And no one understands, or why
He'll build to break and break to build
And never stop till he must die.

Birds Sing
(for two voices)

The birds are whistling, my dear!
No, birds don't whistle after dark.
I tell you it's the birds I hear!
Alright, alright! Perhaps a lark
Is rising up towards a star
Believing it's the sun so far.

But all the birds are singing now,
Blackbird, thrush and nightingale!
No birds are singing where the plough
Lies rusting and there fall, like hail,
Our bitter tears on the grave
Of buried hopes we could not save.

Why can't you hear? The birds repeat
Their song of praise of another light.
Birds sing triumph, I hear defeat.
For we who huddle in this night
Whisp'ring of longings in despair
Can hear no more and will not dare.

But it is, it is the birds
I hear! No, no that dream is lost.
And they mean only what they cost
In lies and truth. And so we pay
Over and over, day after day.

They are singing, singing, I swear!
But on a bough of memory,
A wanton wish, perhaps, is fair,
But night is dark reality
And no birds sing and never shall,
There are no birds to sing in hell.

They sing so sweetly! Do not sing.
The blinds are drawn, the windows shut,
No one comes to the door to bring
Glad tidings. Our pillow is the butt
Of rifles and our sleep the end.
All that's broken we cannot mend.
They sing! No, no, the joy has gone.
The tree in which they sang fell down
Withered at the root when no sun shone.
The other tree now boasts its crown,
Blossoms into death and bells ring
Cracked in the hot winds. Still they sing!

For You and You

For you and you what does your heart beat down,
Down all the rivers of the blood
To the ten tribes of the fingers,
To the wise men of the head?
What read you in the signal smoke of breath?

For you and you what message in the drumming,
Drumming of your pulse and the lighting
Of beacon fires in your cheeks?
What says the orator of passion
Speaking the rhetoric of your eyes?

For you and you what is your true god crying,
Crying in the jungle of your ear?
What fear walks in your dark shadow
That no modern magic can dispel?
O, what dies in chains on your road to hell?

The Search

Through deserted streets,
As Oedipus lame,
A man came limping
And calling a name.
Ghosts of the city cried,
'Who are you calling for?'
Mocked his footsteps as they died,
'Calling for, calling for'.

A harlot detached
Herself from the arms
Of a long lost love
And cried, showing her charms
Under a love torn gown,
'Who are you looking for?'
Came an echo through the town,
'Looking for, looking for'.

At the church he stopped
And called the name.
Through portals of stone
A dead man came
Asking with lips of gold,
'Who are you crying for?'
The bells ironically tolled,
'Crying for, crying for'.

Called the man again
And the night sky wept
For pity of him
And a frail child crept
To touch his hand and said,
'Who are you searching for?'
Repeated the child who is dead,
'Searching for, searching for'.

He turned and limped on
Still calling the name.
A statue of truth,
Forged out of a flame,
Was incessantly crying,
'No one has passed this way'
Called the empty street lying,
'Passed this way, passed this way'.

Then from street to street
His call was sounded,
An echo of despair
By silence hounded.
Outside the city wall
He cried, 'It never shall be found'
From the desert came a call,
'Shall be found, shall be found'.

Disappearing Man

The day grows old with waiting,
Rain falls through withered trees
Slowly, weary with such sorrow
Of a million funeral years.

The sky is dark as slating
On the roofs of houses where
Men lived and live still waiting
For their cancer or despair.

Or in loneliness discover
How each second on each second
Drags out like men forced marching
To a goal that can't be reckoned.

You hear outside your silence
The noises of the city
Where strangers talk with strangers
And communicate no pity.

You pace the room imprisoned
In the bare cell of yourself
Where claustrophobic terror
Has the empty face of grief.

You look into the mirror
And see the self you're seeing
An oddment you've misplaced
A refugee from being.

What are you man whose model
Is repeated and repeated
From conception through deception
To a knowledge you're defeated?

And every man is common
Amongst the millions of his kind,
His nakedness pathetic
Even to his eyes so blind.

So where have you gone to man
Who boasted a god writ large?
From desert to grain of sand
To a complimentary mirage.

The Stain

The shape of my beginning? Listen friend!
A dirty mark on the wall, you know
A stain, a dark discolouring
That from the bricks and mortar seeped through
The dead pan surface of a pastel shade
Distemper, a few chips here and there
And you have a character, a fall.
Use your imagination, trace the shades and lines,
Merge them all into a picture.
What d'you think? A dirty word, a scrawl?
It adds up to something or perhaps
Nothing more than a man's illusion
Of his kind. Anyway you've begun,

It's easy then once you've made a start,
Its all there in the hidden heart
The pathos and the bathos, the drama
And the song.

As Far as I have Come to Stay

After so many years of journeyings
Through barren lands, arrivals and departures,
Expectations and promises hope devised
To lure my reluctant sceptic on
I stand now surveying what can only be
The destination hope was charged to guide me to.

Of course, it could be that I'm just tired,
Tired of trying and would settle for any place
Being here at the end of my tether,
Knowing I can go no further to find
Nothing in the ultimate impasse of despair.
But I do not know and shall never know now
In question and answer sense answers to these
Questions of impossibility.
And yet this is as far as I go

For I see no more signs to lead me
And hope is quiet, as though at last content
To leave me be, no longer whispering
Tomorrow, perhaps further on or teasing me
With dreams or visions my fool cannot resist.
This is as far as I have come to stay
And because I will not, cannot go
Here is beautiful and permanent while I stay
And live.

Initiation

Though there was nothing, nothing there
The boy went into the darkness
Calling, crying, 'show yourself, come out
Of your hiding hole for me to see!'
'Come out, come out, show yourself and be!'
There was no answer, no word, no revelation,
Only a boy calling down the ancient, immeasurably ancient dark.

We could have told him, told him how
We, too, had desperately believed,
Wanting, needing answers to our calls.
Could have told him of the death we died
And how, like our fathers we had lied.
But we gave no word, no sign, no intimation
Saying, 'the nights are drawing in,
There'll be a frost' and smiled, even smiled.

He too, arranged, arranged his life
Within the little lighted square,
Forgot the darkness and who was there,
Told his lies and waited for his son
To search the darkness and call the name
And then return marked with our despair
Crying, 'there is nothing, nothing there!'
So passing his initiation.

Resolution

Young ago
I batted at the tombstone wicket
Unafraid and played
A miracle with my strokes of luck,
Held delight through the dark night
In the arms of my winning ways,
And scorning dull envy's warning
Spent gaily the fortune of my days.

Squawking crow,
High nagger in the summer branches
I have heard no bird
Of dreamers sing sweetly ever since!
Have I learned to be or earned
The bread to keep my being whole?
Believer were you self deceiver
And were the stars insolvent that you stole?

Rivers flow
Between their springs and consummation!
Burning time, like lime,
Leaves only the shades of those who fall!
I shall remember and engender
From the loins of my failure visions
To keep faith, beyond my wrath,
And hate, and hold my heart to their decisions.

The Birth

From out of her distress
She called him.
With a mother's tenderness
She called him.
From evening until morning
She waited, calling, calling
His name until the echo
Came back again
In the ebb and flow
Of tides of pain.

And struggling she went
To find him,
Drowning in tides bent
To find him.
Through doubting and believing
She went on searching, searching
The tempestuous sea
That flung her flesh
On rocks of mercy
She would not bless.

In the fury of the storm
She called him.
In the witch wind's scream and moan
She called him.
In the rising and the falling
Of wild waves heaving, heaving
She gasped and called his name
And through the storm
Answering her he came
Forth to be born.

The Clown

Alley wise with a wishbone
Dreaming the world is kind.
David with a sling of laughter,
Tasting sweetness in the rind.
You're St George upon the dragon
Being taken for a ride.

Dressed up like a child
Serious to pretend
With a hero in each eye
You cannot quite descend
And still holding to a dream
You muff each worldly deed.

O how you would succeed
If only the snob slick trick
Success was friendly,
If you had no love to pick
A flower from the briar,
To release the worm beneath the rock!

And cocking a snoot with you
We ride the donkey of our pride
Through fields of laughter,
A lump in the throat of love
For the changling child we hide
And cannot restore to live.

The Mirage

Thirsting, the first day
He was lost in the wilderness
He cried for water and the way.
Hearing the echoing words
Fill the ear of silence and cry
Hope high to the burning sky.
And in a mirage he saw a tree
Trailing its branches in cool streams
And rooted in the earth's deep sleep
Fulfilling in fruit its green dreams.

When the second day became
A cup of time, baked and glazed
In the potteries of the sun
He cried for water in the name
Of life and dropping in the dust,
To kneel in some forgotten trust,
He wept and kissed the sand
That was salt to his thirst, and with
The obituary silence
Honoured the dead who shall live.

The third day, stumbling the way
Of his thirsting, he saw far on,
Chaliced in the hands of the dead brown
Land, a sacrament of water
And towards the place like a thief,
To steal the treasures of belief,
He went across the cynical sands
With his slowing steps dry laughter
Mocking his envisaging gaze
And the mumbled word of his praise.

To a Child

Dear Child, do not laugh or gurgle with delight,
Only cry and struggle in the sad dark night,
Nourish your pain on the soured breast
Of a generation harnessed to a quest
To find a means to wipe out all the rest.

Sweet child, do not smile and stretch your arms towards the sky
But make ready your unawakened soul to die
For man's devised that from the cloudless sky above
Shall fall a subtle rain of creeping unclean death
On all those people you would have learned to love.

Healthy child, do not dream of sleeping beneath the stars
But work out schemes to hide your face from Mars.
In excavations, as deep as fear can make you go,
Huddle yourself ready for the cosmic blow,
Dealt, in panicky suspicion, by friend or foe.

Faithful child, do not let your heart beat strong
To passionately examine right or wrong
Because justice, even of the kind that they
Who with glib minds reasoned it away,
Left this world on Hiroshima's judgement day.

Tender child, do not stare with rapture at the flowers
Or think that you will spend with Nature simple hours;
Harden your heart to the trembling pity of their plea,
Forget the beauty and extract ruthlessly the seed,
It may contain a means to achieve a fouler deed.

Artistic child, do not gaze with expectation
At the wonder of your hands, their realisation
Will be lost in horrified covers for your face
Or clasped, perhaps, in unlearned prayers of a bygone race
As you, with sickening fear, cross an open space.

Trusting child, do not look with innocent belief
Into eyes that stare in horror and in grief
But condemn as unproved that which you have not
known,
Call propaganda even the proofs you're shown,
Destroy the other's truth and then distrust your own.

Loving child, don't let your fierce love express
Its full treasure in all mankind to bless
But distort its beauty and deform its shape
Into hideous caricatures that mock and ape;
Until there's no returning and no escape.

Living child, count not life to be the great reward
But thrust into your heart annihilation's sword
And find in death the wish fulfilment of the blessed
Who hasten to a crimson setting in the west
And with themselves wipe out all the rest.

Shall Fall

We held on,
You know we held on,
Even as we fell.
Yes, even when,
When there was nothing,
Nothing there to hold
We tried – we –
But you also knew
The terror, the fall,
Hands screaming to claw,
Hate, love and all
Breaking to dust
And the last thought dumb.
After? But now is after
The fall a long time.
Born from the saved dead
We began again.
You smile,
Smirk your laboratory smile.
Can't you remember?
Won't you remember
The scream ebbing
To a mouth's dribble
And the whimpering, why?
Then,
The eyes breaking
Open to the stars' night?

Now of course
It seems such a little thing,
That death or birth,
Awakening or dream.
And yet today
It troubles me, as though

It was an event
I should remember
And forget, to bear
Witness in some trial to come
When even your proud advocate
Shall fall and be dumb.

The Exchange

Oh yes, I am the finest cook, she said.
I know a recipe for making bread
To feed the living and the dead.
I know a means to transmute lead
Into the purest gold, he said.
They smiled, together we would be complete,
Invulnerable against our own defeat.
They exchanged knowledge of each other,
The realist mistress and alchemist lover.
But the gold he made her changed back to lead
And the bread she baked left him unfed.

Nothing to Report

After the long looking
I have nothing to report,
Though the smell of cooking
On hungry days has taught
Me how to bless. And where
Beyond I could not go
I have turned around to share
That which we cherish because we know.

I have nothing to report
For I have found nothing new.
All that I needed and brought
With me I can return to you,
Travelled and worn but intact.
They have stood their test and more.
What I did not find I lacked
And there's no weeping on the far shore.

Having nothing to report
No one will want to know,
Nor care, why I went or brought
Nothing back. So dust will blow
Over the years that have passed.
But those I left behind
And have lost in the vast
Void of my neglect; shall I find?

No Ending

He did not say, you cannot!
He let me try
And I
Made the first incision
Feeling no pain.

So simple it seemed to take
Out of my side
The pride
Of the human condition
To mould in my hands.

As simple as arrogance!
So I began,
A man
With a boy's hands trembling
In skilless endeavour

To create from the first clay
Over again
The pain
Into the shape of love
His truth envisaged.

Articled then to my trade
I caught my days
In ways
Of the word's dimension
To suffer out thought.

Practising every failure,
The imperfect
Perfect
Unknowing trial by death
Of all life living,

I began a beginning
With no ending;
Sending
Me back to the starting
Place in the killing

World of my murdering hands
That must redeem
The dream,
Given in the first trust
To make manifest.

The Question

I wake in the night's dark
And count my heart's rhythm
Against the bedside clock.
It beats a strict, measured
Fifty eight times a minute.
I ask myself this question.
Is this perpetual motion pump,
This clenching fist of muscle
The oyster wherein the grit
Of love and hate produces
The pearl of life?

After Pubs Close

After pubs close
After smart talk
And warm smiles
The friendly touch
And generous "what's yours"
The hasty "goodnights"
In the cold windy alley
And the harrying away
To smuggeries or huggeries
You are alone and known
Only to the cynic wind
And contemptuous dark
And the grinning moon
Jesting between clouds
At your haunched shoulders
And hands deep in pockets
Feeling comforts of small change
With the fallen arches
Of your athletic smiles
Past prime and triumph
You kick a loose stone
Savagely and take
Another cigarette to make
Ashes of burning
Climb in your car
Race the engine loudly
Lacerate the tyres
On the drive's sharp gravel
And roar away cavalier
As not caring.

The Yield

The yield of yesteryear
I gather at the heart's harvest!
Cornflower smile and thistle tear,
Breath that blew the blow-clock to
Love's hour shall not be lost,
And with the sweat and pain it cost
I load a laugh with luxuries,
The wheat that makes the golden bread,
The apple from the springing tree,
The dream unwounded and unshed.

Wine I've pressed from lips of grape
I hold up to the evening light
And see again the summer shape
Full flesh ripe in the burning eye
Of sun, grain gold and garnered green;
Old men unmeaning but to lean
Against the comfort of their years
Make pipe peace with what they think,
And furred and feathered lovers go
Down to the pure pool to drink.

Galloping on Hope's high horse,
Spurred and booted in my faith,
I race the river down its course
To where the sea of Time defends
My island from the unknown foe;
On my face I feel the blow
Of the word's wind from lips of gods
Conversing through infinity,
And spat spray stings my eyes to tears
For salted with love is the sea

Wine-washed my tongue tastes truth
And drunk on deeply I become,
Crier at the fairground booth
Extolling wonder of the world,
Heretic priest who prays
Night into a tower of days,
Fool singing winter into spring,
Sower of the sullen seeds
That in some distant Spring will leap
Passionately to flowers of deeds.

A Man Rises

The days grow old with waiting,
Weary at their turn of a century
As the false Cassandra spits
Her prophecies into the wind.

Dawn, noon and sun set weaken
The wings of the highest eagle
Till the slippered moon relaxes
Into its coma of fullness.

A man rises like a god
Amidst the hunchbacked laughter
And silent in his knowledge
Goes out to the urinal.

Part XI: Time

Late Evening Anchorage

At anchor in a harbour's keep,
The breeze a child's breath asleep,
I read the silhouette of trees.
The vaguely disappearing hills,
Like poems of forgotten ways
In quiet revelation held
In the eyes of all my days.

But darkness falls,
The dinghy knocks,
Knocks against the hull,
A night bird calls.
I look for signs of threat;
See none in the lull
Before what comes and must be met.

For This Day

For this day, I say, believe me,
Time turns traitor and betrays.
Tomorrow all that we have wept for
Will be for laughter in comic plays.

For this day we'll pray, no other,
What we ask today tomorrow
Brings, bountiful as garden weeds,
Choking another Spring with sorrow,

For this day delay a little
The forces that destroy and make,
Hold the flaming sword of Eden
In its scabbard for our hearts' sake.

The Face in the Mirror

The bleak face in the mirror looks
Like dead words of forgotten books,
The eyes where promise used to shine
Are grapes from which was trodden wine.

The lips, where laughter took its oath,
Once courted song and made of both
The question and the answer fun
Whisper now, 'if I could have won'.

The mask, like curtains drawn to hide
The grief and agony inside
Still withholds the relieving cry
So no tear falls from either eye.

Spring

And the land was still
No blade of a will
Of grass moved to defend
Its home of earth.
No screaming birth
Suffered out to the end.
No ghost of a death
Was felt, no human breath
Sighed or gasped for love
Or fear. And above,
The blank yawn of the sky
Reigned over all
Of nought. No call
To arms or the stark cry
Of the flesh and pain
Could ever break or stain
With life the dead land.

The seeds in my hand
Vibrate in revolt.
I break the soil,
Blessing the toil
To live, finding no fault
In the rough seasons
Of the heart or reasons
Of the thorn and rose.

Evening Ebb

The seas are held by the magnet moon
From the grey, cold wounded land.
A cormorant, spreading its black hands,
Praises the air with its sudden flight
On the stillness of the world's stopped breath.
The quiet mist creeps in
Where the painted silence holds
Its secrets to its breast.
The boats, withdrawn into themselves,
Lie in contemplation as they wait.
Nothing moves except the coming on
Of haloed harbour lights
To mark the inevitability of night.

For That Old Man

The afternoon ages
In shadows across the lawn
And the fading pages
Of your book appear to yawn.

A bedroom window grins
Almost as though your sins
Are gathering in the room behind
To celebrate the days
When you'd the courage not to mind
The salted whip that flays.

Before the Festival

Before the festival of fools,
The clowning into summer,
All the blossom promise to be broken,
Tender leaves and mockery of making,
Cuckoo and building birds
There come the warnings by frost
Grim as ghosts to frighten
The flowers so young and brazen
Shrivelling into their beds.

Before the blasphemy of birds
In the crucifixion trees
Crowned in resurrection glory up to heaven
And the innocence of lambing and larking
In the newly sudden sun
Burning a hole in the sky's
Blue and spendthrift pocket:
And the clouds in their weeds sorrow
For all unbegotten sons.

At your first breaking to belief
Or prophecy of dreams
Of love lasting more than a season to say
A wind's whisper to move a mountain of sand,
Call the catechism
Of the unloved in the ward
Of murder and of rape,
Within the ancient temple
Before the altar of praise.

No Witness Needed

Even in the call days of my wanting,
In the new summer with the sun too soon
Conning the blossom out of bud,
Before the apple was set in its Adam ways
I dreamed of this, not knowing how it could be.
And now, nearly in my fiftieth year,
An age of settling the odds or looking back
On all the half successes adding up to failure,
I have begun the beginning of a youth,
Holding my head high and calling my truth.
I know, I know so many times I have called
My muse down from the silent singing tower
To bless my earth and witness how the Spring
Thawed my winter blood to return in flood.
This time I need not call a witness to
Sign my affidavit and swear its truth.
The streams are running and over full,
The blossom breaks and the fruit is set.
This summer's promised and cannot fall.
One swallow makes no summer, this I've learned,
But two's enough to call the winter past,
To trick the sleeping flowers out of snow
And court the wiser trees, who always know,
Real summer's not prophesied by time
But always is
When leaves in the sun are green.

The Day goes without Comment

The day goes without comment
From the thoughtless idling hours
For there is nothing to lament
Except what time devours.

Old age has a taste like blood
That is sucked out of the soul;
A reckoning before the flood,
Words on an unwritten scroll.

A safe house is offered you
But you're given no address
And you know that nothing true
Comes from a wild and wishful guess.

So you wait and just accept,
Like animals in the Ark,
A something that must be met
When ushered into the dark.

The Comedy was Yesterday

Of course the comedy was yesterday
The bitterness, the pain and love so out of date
Sharpens up the laughs
Of the new wise shaking their golden heads
And expounding their unlearned philosophy,
Unearned their sweetened bread, their wine
Unmade from miracles of water
And their first stone cast
By no muscled righteousness
Their laughter lives
On the comedy of yesterday,
The tragedy's to come!
The bitterness, the pain, the out of date
Unloveliness
And all the decaying smiles
Remembering no tears to minus sympathy
In seminars of the heart.

Sonnet in Old Age

Remembering, like film in black and white,
Has muted voices and grainy faces,
Disconnected scenes and unnamed places
And up the wooden hill by candlelight
To dancing shadows and forgotten fears.
That boy, that man of long ago is now
A stranger who unwittingly appears
Lumbering in like an awkward sacred cow
On some known street, its name you can't recall,
Jogging old faiths you long since out of hand
Rejected after your own special fall.
Accusing witnesses then take the stand,
Old foes, old friends and those who broke your heart
In court where only you the judgements hurt.

Old Poet's Lament

What can I say more than I've said before?
Have I the need to turn another trick?
A useless gesture like an old street whore
Plying her trade in the night of the sick.
Yet in habit I take my pen again
To best the doubter that lies within,
That raw intransigent, uncultured lout
Who sneers at every pretentious whim.
Hell, I only use language in a way
To make my naked thoughts presentable.
At my life's age I can't a new game play
And the old one is incomparable
Having that profoundly human imprint
Of love's immortal brutal sentiment.

On the Last Day

And on the last day
The sun shall rise,
The brass cock slay
Silence with its cosh of cries
And the divisions of liberating light
Come marching down the mountain sides,
Driving before them the vanquished night.

A bride shall pick the rose
And in her hair
The red, red rose
Of love and hate will be more fair;
And blessing the day that brings belief
Through all the happy omens that portend
Such future joy, she'll see no sign of grief.

A murderer shall fail to kill,
The heart disclose
The natural will
Of man to harvest what he sows,
And in the cities crowds shall go their way
Pursuing what their hope predicts
Shall come tomorrow to forgive today.

Men shall discover peace,
A child be born,
A war shall cease
And none shall bow his head nor mourn
On the last day when every silenced bell
Shall peal as though for victory
And the release of prisoners from hell.

And on the final day
The sun shall set,
Dusk kneel to pray,
Night fish with her magic net
For stars to feed the hungry dreamers with
While the moon, as grave as wisdom, journeys forth
To greet the first day eternity shall give.

Part X: Think of this Poet

Think of this Poet

Think of this poet.
A late comer to the great spectacle
Of earth and heaven:
Listening to the first songs still sung by
Birds and rivers
And the laughing and weeping seasons,
Being with rhythms
Of seas and skies and stars in their ever
Striving to gather
Windfalls from the gloried tree of heaven.

And awakening
In a world wondered into a word
To be spoken,
That ever the shot through the lungs wind
Struggles to speak
And the rain grizzles down in all the old
Cold frustrations
Of winter and pain and passing over.
As the new born cry
In the protest of their first sobbing breath.

To be man and maker,
Knowing the tumbling down of girls in the
High hay heaven.
Sweat of breaking the cold side of the sun
And of the taking
And the giving back to eyes their visions
And to hearts their love;
Until the stars are hotter mouths to kiss
And the singing bird,
Escaping from the cage, discovers trees and sky.

Making a Poem

To me a poem comes when the first gift lines
Smile into my head
Like my wife across a room at parties
Making me feel good all evening,
Valued in a world of strangers.
I wait, unthinking and yet willing
The words to speak again and listening
Hear a voice as though reciting
From the turned page of an unwritten volume,
And each line that follows called out from where
My mind is bound like wisps of mist
To the opaque surface of lake water
Very early on a Sunday, sunny morning.

Forty Summers

Birds, summer full bellied, sing
And fling their reckless flight,
Like laughter of the light,
Down the warmly dozing summer air.
And dimpled daydreams throng
Along the avenues of the young
Hoping and provoking their ways to be wise,
Not with the thin winter wisdom
Of the brain but of the blood and the bud
And the fruit famous with their legends of love
And laughter, song and will to be strong.
O sing sluggard senses, sing!
Sing with the wind in the leaves,
With the wild word
Shy to the tongue

Of the pedant dusting his vowels
And consonants in the lumber room year
And bear on a song the world,
Radiant from the lips of girls
Gathering honey of kisses to praise
This shining and begetting time.

O mating and making undone!
One dream was not enough to hold.
It told only half the story,
Undressed the naked of their shame
And blessed them back to children
To try again to begin the whole story.

Give me, glory of living, my life
Back into my hands to make
And mould into a shape of flesh
And blood and heart to beat
So strongly in its love to wake
The seven sleepers on the Elysian shore
So they shall sing into my mind
A singing where my tongue is dumb,
A seeing where my eyes are blind.

Rhythm

The rhythm of sleep and dreams
Reasons out of the mind
The day to day thinking
And makes miracles of meaning,
Poetry of prose.

Self Doubt

Am I losing my nerve for words
After so many deeds of poems?
Three months dumb as an oyster!
I drift on a calm sea
Not daring to dive to the bottom
To search my dumbness for pearls.

I must go down, cleanly over the side
And not rock the boat with my doubt and fear
For after my dive I will need a steady boat
To return to, which ever I find;
A pearl when I open my dumbness
Or emptiness, the constant dread of my kind.

Dictation

I sit down on empty evenings
And read the poems I have written
Over the long life years
And wonder from where they come.
The eureka thoughts tumbling
On to the tongue from a million voices
Still echoing through the space of the past
And taken down like dictation
Half understood, as by a pupil
Listening to a teacher in a rowdy classroom.

Mutation

And they joined and made me,
Sealing in the cell
Their gifts I cannot break
Despite the years of stones
I pile to crush them.

The message that inside
They wrote to guide me
I repeat ten million times
But cannot say more than
Its meaning gave me.

And yet, perhaps, there was
A stutter or missing word
And in that gap I'll write
A new word men shall cry
To live, and recreate me.

Not Heard

I cry out, scream, rage and am not heard,
Talk tender, tough, or arrogant as tears
Shed by gods in frustration against laws
Of universal immutability,
Fool my words into saying
More than they can quite believe,
But I am not heard.
Is my tongue too twisted to be untied,
A schizophrenic coding without a key,
Or a one-man jargonese to con
This one follower into pretensions?
Am I a deaf mute stumbling in the dark silence,
Bubbling noises painful as wounds
In the fair flesh of the articulate?
I hear myself calling and the beautiful echoes back
Through the deep valley of my consciousness.
The blackbird and the nightingale
Sing not only for their vanity
And pleasure unshared is a sour wine
Making a melancholy drunkard.
Yet when I sometimes listen down the years
I hear the singing of the poems I have made
And wonder how the silence held so long
Unbroken by the agony of them.

Note to Myself

Three months, two months, too long
To hear no word from I,
Has communication ceased,
Or the lines been cut
By the enemy in me?
I wait and wait with dreams
Of suffocation but the word of breath
Is still unspoken and unheard.
There are other men, I know,
Who all their lives, since children,
Have stopped their word
Deliberate as lobotomy
Or perversely gagged the mouth
That spoke the word they could not hear.
It is a way of coping
And for them must be.
But any man who's listened
Through the long night
Silence of himself
And caught the singing word
Faintly through the thicknesses
Of nothing and the blanks of nought,
The pure voice in word,
Clearly, though a whisper,
Above the babbling talk of thought,
Counts himself as chosen,
One with the right to hear.
Yet two months, three months?
Humility, perhaps, is needed more.
No! Humility is invested in the right,
The apprenticeship of waiting
And the creation of hearing what is heard.
The fool is wiser than the clever man
For fools have faith the clever can't divine.
Fool take this note to yourself
Listen and you will hear yourself speak.

I Must Get Away

I must get away from prying eyes
And all the dreams that were never meant
For more than wrapping round false gifts.
Escape from where my beating heart
Is heard as vulgar and too loud,
From where my free but tattered tongue
Is asked to array itself so neat
And perjure all its wildest truth.
Must get away and count no more
Abortive Springs and barren Summers
With their blossoms of white lies
That bear the fruit of nothingness,
Must get away and count the days
And add them up to what I am,
A man with poet's need to say.

Voices

All the voices of the world
Calling through centuries of song
With the poet's wondering word
If you listen can be heard
In the whispers of leaves,
In the roar of oceans
And in the patient sighs of our
Most impatient breath.
Truth waiting to be sold,
Striving to he heard;
Aching like a suppressed orgasm
In the loins of language;
A voice in the background of the mind
Calling out like hidden revelation,
Calling, calling and rarely heard.

The New Man

He'll be alone
Along the dark way
No light but his own
Moods creating day
And night, his husbandry in the heart's seasons
Perfunctory
For he'll be listening
To the faint cry calling him past reasons.

He'll hear the word
Winging through a dream,
Like a wild bird
Whose song must seem
The apocalypse to the sightless worm
And feel the longing and the urgency
As, for birth, must the still unchosen sperm.

And somewhere on,
Through the fissure
Of imagination
He'll creep like wonder
In a child and conceive and bring forth himself
To walk upright under the sun,
A prince of all the dominions of belief.

So to be born
Every man was made
Holding the horn
Of plenty. And unafraid,
No longer with his heart in his mouth of time,
He'll tongue from curses and from praise
Songs of water into wine.

When the First Man Spoke

When the first man spoke
Poetry was born
Down the ages and pages
Of the hallowed word.
Formed by the grace of the longhand's ink
To the music of the thought's sounds,
Moulded with the tongue's passion to speak
In parables of beauty and truth
And reveal the promise of innocence.

O! The gift line, given out of the blue
Of a clear sky on a dreaming day.
Plucked like a jewel from a pit's slag heap
In the freedom of a moment that escaped the hour.
Not God's word but the word of man
From the sages and wages
Of our common speech.
From all those voices down the generations of the word
A message to the poet who can listen
Humbly: before his own conceits.

Come the Day when You are Older

Written at the Arvon Foundation
Totleigh Barton 29-11-05

Come the day when you are older,
And bereft of words within your mind
You will look back on all
The poems you have written
And wonder why they break your heart
And then you'll know why
You became a poet, not for fame
Or that fool's gold ambition
But for the manhood that made you stand
Naked before the world
And proclaim your love
For life in all its glory and its shame.

Index of Poems

Acknowledgements

'A little loving', *Leicester Mercury*, 1968; *Child Care News*, 1969
'After pubs close', *Leicester Mercury*, 1968
'Between losing and finding', *Child Care News*, 1973
'Dead end', *Tribune*, 1964; *Leicester Mercury*, 1969
'Doorman's resignation', *The Listener*, 1957
'Enlightenment', *Leicester Mercury*, 1967
'Explanation', *Child Care News*, 1967
'Initiation', *Child Care News*, 1968
'Miner's death', *New Statesman*, 1954
'On the last day', *New Statesman*, 1953
'Poet miner', *New Statesmann*, 1953
'Portsmouth Harbour (8.45pm, 7th June 1971)', *This Island City*, Spinnaker Press, 2010
'Postcard from here', *Child Care News*, 1969
'Rising for the early shift', *Leicester Mercury*, 1969
'The clown', *Daily Express*, 1963
'The disciple', *Tribune*, 1964
'The last romantic', *Tribune*, 1964; *Child Care News*, 1969
'The new man', *New Statesman*, 1955
'The search', *The Listener*; *Harpers Bazaar* (USA); read on BBC Radio 3, 1942/3
'The trial', *The Listener*, 1955
'The way', *The Listener*, 1956
'The Widower', *Leicester Mercury*, 1968; *The Lady*, 1982; Read on 'Poetry Please' BBC Radio 4, 2005
'The Yield', *The Listener*, 1954
'Voice in a dream', *The Listener*, 1955
'Waiting to Descend', *Observer Weekend Review*, 1966
'We passed through Nazareth', *The Listener*, 1951
'What would I have done?', *AJR*, July 2010
'You'd think spring would make a difference', *Leicester Mercury*, 1968

Most of the poems in this collection were included in *Waiting to Descend*, Sarsen Press, Winchester, 2006